A THEORY OF
PROFITS

ADRIAN WOOD

*Fellow of King's College, Cambridge
and University Lecturer in Economics*

CAMBRIDGE UNIVERSITY PRESS

CAMBRIDGE

LONDON · NEW YORK · MELBOURNE

Published by the Syndics of the Cambridge University Press
The Pitt Building, Trumpington Street, Cambridge CB2 1RP
Bentley House, 200 Euston Road, London NW1 2DB
32 East 57th Street, New York, NY 10022, USA
296 Beaconsfield Parade, Middle Park, Melbourne 3206, Australia

First published 1975

Printed in Great Britain
at the
University Printing House, Cambridge
(Euan Phillips, University Printer)

Library of Congress Cataloguing in Publication Data
Wood, Adrian.
  A theory of profits
  Bibliography: p. 175
  Includes index.
  1. Profit. I. Title
HB601. W84   338.5'16   75-2725
ISBN: 0 521 20768 1

CONTENTS

PREFACE

Inevitably, much of this book will be incomprehensible to anyone who is not an economist. But I have tried to write it in such a way that other readers will be able to grasp both the basic ideas which it contains and the implications of those ideas for government policy. This has led me, among other things, to make more use of footnotes than is customary. First, in order to reduce to a minimum the amount of mathematics in the text, I have provided quite a number of mathematical footnotes designed to clarify particular points. I have also endeavoured to answer in footnotes certain criticisms and questions that I anticipate will arise in the minds of economists at specific points in the text. Finally, I have also used footnotes in the usual way to provide cross-references and to undertake minor digressions.

My intellectual debts, which are considerable, are described in general terms in the third section of the first chapter. More specifically, I owe a very great deal to Professor N. Kaldor and Dr R. L. Marris, whose work both inspired my interest in the subject of this book and provided the starting point for my own analysis. In the course of writing the book, however, I have come to disagree with them in a number of important respects, and they cannot be held responsible for its contents. The same is true, of course, of the other people who have been so kind as to read and comment on earlier drafts, of whom I would particularly like to thank Professor A. B. Atkinson, Professor D. G. Champernowne, Dr C. R. S. Dougherty, Mr W. A. H. Godley, Professor F. H. Hahn, Professor G. C. Harcourt, Professor R. F. Kahn, Mr M. A. King, Dr J. M. Malcomson, Professor Joan Robinson, Mr J.-C. Sailly and Mr M. C. Wolfson.

ADRIAN WOOD

Cambridge
July 1974

TERMINOLOGY

American readers should be warned that this book uses words in their British senses. In particular, what are called 'stocks' in this book are called 'inventories' in the U.S., while what are called 'shares' in this book are called 'stocks' in the U.S.

1

INTRODUCTION

1.1 A THEORY OF PROFITS

The purpose of this book is to explain what determines the profit margin of the individual firm and the share of profits in national income. This is a subject to which economists have addressed themselves for at least two hundred years, but without much success. For there is at the moment no general theory of profits which commands anything approaching universal acceptance either among academic economists or among men of affairs. Instead, there are a number of different schools of thought, between which there is a considerable amount of disagreement. The fact, therefore, that the present theory belongs to none of the main schools of economic thought should perhaps be counted among its merits. For although in a certain sense it is not a new theory, and although it inevitably overlaps with other theories, it would be misleading to characterise it as a 'neoclassical' or a 'neo-Keynesian' or a 'degree of monopoly' theory. Indeed, in order to make clear the nature of the present theory, quite a lot of space will be devoted to discussing the respects in which it differs from other theories.

But before plunging into a theoretical discussion it is essential to state exactly what it is that the present theory is intended to explain. By 'profits' we shall mean the gross trading profits of privately owned industrial and commercial companies.* That is,

---

* Most of the concepts and definitions in this book correspond with those used both in British company accounts and in the British national accounts; see *National Income and Expenditure*, and Maurice (1968). Where, however, the conventions of company accountants and national accountants diverge, we shall follow the former, since these are the basis on which companies make decisions. The principal example of such a divergence at the present time concerns the measurement of investment in stocks. Company accountants measure this as the change in the value of stocks while national accountants measure it as the change in the volume of stocks valued at current prices. The difference between the two measures is called 'stock appreciation' ('inventory valuation adjustment' in the U.S.); see Maurice (1968) ch. XIII. The magnitude of stock appreciation depends primarily on (a) the way in

profits will be measured gross of interest payments, taxation and depreciation provisions, but net of non-trading income (such as interest on financial assets owned by companies), and we shall exclude the 'profits' of nationalised industries, financial companies and unincorporated businesses. Nationalised industries and financial companies are excluded because, from the viewpoint of the present theory, their behaviour is fundamentally different from that of privately owned industrial and commercial companies. The same is true of most unincorporated businesses, especially those which are small and those in which not much capital is employed. But the present theory, with minor modifications, would apply to large unincorporated industrial and commercial businesses; we exclude them merely for convenience, because in quantitative terms they are of minor importance in modern capitalist economies.

It is also worth noting that the present theory is intended primarily to provide an explanation of the *long run* profit margin of the individual firm and of the *long run* share of profits in national income. The precise meaning of the term 'long run' will be considered below; at this point it is simplest to define it in terms of a three-to-five year moving average. We shall not altogether neglect short run (i.e. year-to-year) movements of the profit margin and the share of profits, but they will receive relatively little attention in this book because they are a phenomenon whose cause is already comparatively well understood. Economists have been unable, however, to agree on what governs the trend about which these short run fluctuations occur, and it is this unresolved issue that is our main concern.

Finally, it should perhaps be pointed out that the present theory,

which company accountants value stocks and (b) the extent to which the prices at which stocks are purchased vary from year to year. At present company accountants in Britain value stocks on a 'first in, first out' basis; as a result, in periods of inflation investment in stocks as measured by company accountants is significantly greater than investment in stocks as measured by national accountants. The measurement of investment in stocks is closely bound up with the measurement of profits, since profits are defined as sales revenue minus operating costs where operating costs are defined as current outlays minus investment in stocks. As far as the *principles* of the present theory are concerned it is of no importance how company accountants measure investment in stocks, although the theory implies that this may affect the size both of the profit margin of the individual firm and of the share of profits in national income – see pp. 62n, 67n, 98n, 107 and 168.

which deals with the profit margin (profits as a ratio of sales revenue) and with the share of profits in national income, could quite easily be reformulated in terms of the profit *rate* (profits as a ratio of the value of the capital stock), which is from some theoretical points of view a more useful sort of variable.* This alternative approach was not adopted for two reasons. First, the valuation of capital stocks involves numerous practical difficulties, and thus profit rates are in a statistical sense less satisfactory variables than profit margins and profit shares. Secondly, and more fundamentally, the main object of the book is to provide an explanation of the distribution of income.

It cannot be claimed, however, that this book is exclusively concerned with income distribution; indeed, I believe that it throws light on several aspects of company behaviour. Nor can it be claimed that this book deals with more than one dimension of income distribution. Very little is said, for example, about the distribution of profits among individual persons (which depends on the inter-personal distribution of certain sorts of property as well as on the share of profits in national income), and nothing is said about the distribution of wages and salaries among individual persons, or about the incomes of those people who live on transfers from the government.† Thus the present theory, while it is addressed to that dimension of income distribution which has always been the main concern of economists, bears only to a limited extent on the causes of wealth and poverty in the sense in which those terms are used in common speech.

I.2 PROFITS, GROWTH AND FINANCE

The essential principles of the present theory are very simple. Nonetheless, economists (particularly those of the neoclassical school)‡ may find them difficult to understand. This is because orthodox economics excludes by assumption certain features of the real world which are central to the present theory. But before

---

* In connection with a reformulation of this kind see pp. 98, 121, and 126 below.

† Nor are profits in the present sense the same thing as 'income from property' or 'surplus value.'

‡ I.e. the school which includes such economists as Marshall, Walras, Fisher and Debreu.

we can elaborate on this proposition we must attempt a preliminary statement of the theory.

The chief object of the typical firm in a capitalist economy is to cause its sales to grow. This entails the expansion of its productive capacity, which in turn requires investment in fixed assets and stocks. The firm must, of course, be able to finance this investment; that is, it must be able to obtain the funds needed for expenditure on its capital projects. In practice, ploughed-back profits are necessarily the main source of finance for investment. The central principle of the present theory, therefore, is that the amount of profits which the firm sets out to earn is determined by the amount of investment that it plans to undertake.

Naturally enough, there are restrictions on the individual firm's desire to invest. In particular, competition from other firms limits both the rate of expansion of its sales and its ability to make profits. But at this stage of the argument the essential point to grasp is that the level of profits is determined by the need to finance a particular level of investment. For this causal link is the basis on which we shall construct both a model of the determination of the profit margin of the individual firm and a model of the determination of the share of profits in national income.

There are a number of reasons why the present theory is bound to seem peculiar to neoclassical economists.* The most important of them can be summed up by saying that in neoclassical theory the availability of finance is not a problem for the firm. More precisely, the neoclassical position is that the firm is willing and able to finance by borrowing any investment project that it would be prepared to finance out of retained profits. If this were true in reality the present theory would immediately collapse. For there would be no need whatsoever for the firm to rely on retained profits as a source of finance for investment; as a result, the basis of the present theory would disappear.

It is therefore worth making a closer examination of the neoclassical position. It rests on two sorts of assumptions. The first relates to the motivation of businessmen; the neoclassical assump-

---

* Some of these relate to matters of form alone. For example most neoclassical models assume that firms operate in perfectly competitive markets and thus have no effective control over their profits. But in practice no neoclassical economist would dispute the widespread existence of monopoly power.

tion is that the aim of those in charge of a firm is to maximise the present value of its future earnings ('earnings' being profits in the present sense plus non-trading income minus interest payments, taxation and depreciation provisions). The second sort of assumption concerns the nature of the capital market, and is in turn a consequence of certain assumptions about the degree of knowledge of the future that people possess and about their attitudes towards borrowing and lending.

The easiest way to expound the neoclassical position is in the context of a world of certainty, in which the future outcomes of all events are known to everyone. Let us also assume for simplicity that there are no transactions costs and that the capital market is perfect in the sense that no individual borrower or lender has a perceptible influence on the prevailing interest rate.* A necessary condition for the firm to be prepared to finance an investment project out of retained profits is that its net present value should be positive when discounted at the ruling rate of interest; otherwise the firm would be better off lending the money to someone else. But this condition also ensures that if no retained profits happen to be available the firm will be willing and able to execute the project with borrowed money. It will be willing to borrow because this course of action will increase its earnings; the proceeds of the project will be sufficient to pay the interest and to repay the loan with something to spare. For the same reasons, lenders will have no hesitation in advancing the money because they are secure in the knowledge that the interest will be paid and their principal refunded when the loan matures. A 'finance problem' could arise only with regard to a project whose net present value was negative, but this would be a project which the firm would have no desire to undertake whatever the source of finance. In such a world, then, retained profits are in no sense a necessary source of finance for investment.

No economist would maintain for a moment that the assumption of certainty is realistic. But the basic neoclassical result survives the introduction of uncertainty provided that certain assumptions are made. The most important of these are as follows.

* Which a neoclassical economist would suppose to be determined by the interaction of society's intertemporal preferences and intertemporal invest ment opportunities: see, for example, Dougherty (1972).

(a) Expectations of the future, while uncertain, must be 'objective' in the sense of being common to all agents in the capital market. In other words, everyone must have the same view of the magnitude and uncertainty of the future returns from any particular investment project.

(b) If a firm would be prepared to undertake a project with retained profits (i.e. if the expected rate of return on a project exceeds the prevailing interest rate on loans of what the firm regards as a comparable degree of uncertainty), it must be willing to carry out the project with money borrowed at that particular risk-adjusted interest rate.

(c) Lenders must be willing to provide finance for any investment project provided that the rate of interest on the loan is sufficient to compensate them for what they regard as the degree of uncertainty involved.

By virtue of the first assumption, both lenders and borrowers must have the same opinion as to the particular risk-adjusted interest rate that is appropriate to any specific investment project. Given this, the second and third assumptions ensure that the firm will be willing and able to finance by borrowing any investment project that it would be prepared to finance out of retained profits, which is the essence of the neoclassical position.

Needless to say, all three of these assumptions are wildly misleading. Indeed, they convey an image of the capital market under uncertainty which is unrealistic to the point of almost complete irrelevance. Let us consider each of them in turn.

(a) The problem with the first assumption is that it fails to recognise that in reality expectations are inevitably 'subjective' in the sense that they are specific to the individual and liable to vary among individuals. For different people commonly entertain very different opinions about the magnitude and uncertainty of the future returns from any particular investment project, a fact which not only damages the neoclassical position but also, and more generally, makes it difficult to see how there could be any neat and tidy model of the capital market as a whole. In consequence, borrowers and lenders are unlikely to agree on what rate of interest is appropriate to any given investment project. Thus if, as is frequently the case, potential lenders have a more jaded view than potential borrowers of the prospective returns from particular ventures, a firm may be unwilling to borrow to finance an investment project that it would be prepared to finance out of retained profits. The reason for this is simply that potential lenders may insist on an interest rate so much above that which the firm regards as appropriate to the degree of risk involved as to make it an unattractive proposition to undertake the project with borrowed money.

(b) The problem with the second assumption is that it ignores the fact that borrowing money in an uncertain world is an activity which entails certain risks and disadvantages which do not arise (or only to a much smaller extent) when investment projects are undertaken out of retained profits. These peculiar risks and disadvantages (which will be discussed at greater length in the next chapter) include the possibilities of bankruptcy, of loss of control over the firm and of ruined managerial careers. In consequence there are many cases in which a firm will refuse to borrow money to undertake a particular investment project even if it would be enthusiastic about financing the project out of retained profits (rather than making a loan of a comparable degree of uncertainty) and even if potential lenders are in agreement with the firm about the magnitude and uncertainty of the returns from the project.

(c) The problem with the third assumption is that it neglects the possibility of outright refusals to lend at any interest rate. For beyond a certain point the prospect of a higher interest rate may make potential lenders less willing rather than more willing to lend to a particular firm, because the increased burden of interest payments will add to the risks of the firm defaulting and being forced into bankruptcy in circumstances such as to cause its creditors to lose part or all of their money. In practice, therefore, loans are made only if the borrowing firm can provide security in the form of easily realisable assets on which there are no other claims; the prospect of future profits does not normally constitute adequate collateral. Thus there are circumstances in which a firm is unable to borrow money to undertake a particular project even if it would be willing to do so and even if potential lenders share the firm's opinions about the prospective returns from the project.

Finally, let us abandon the neoclassical assumption about business motivation. For it appears to me to be untrue to say that the typical firm in a capitalist economy is concerned primarily to maximise the present value of its earnings. A much more accurate assumption, which will be maintained throughout this book, is that the basic goal of those in charge of the firm is to cause its sales revenue to grow as rapidly as possible. For there is a considerable body of evidence which suggests that businessmen are forever striving to increase the size of their firms, and sales revenue appears to be the most widely used measure of size.* Of course, businessmen are by no means unconstrained in their pursuit of growth; indeed, a great deal will be said in later chapters about the nature of the constraints under which they operate.

But for the present it is sufficient to note that the fact that the firm's aim is to maximise the growth of its sales rather than the present value of its earnings inflicts further damage on the neoclassical view of finance. This is because it becomes likely that there will be investment projects which the firm would be keen to finance out of retained profits but which have a negative net present value when discounted at the interest rate that the firm could obtain if it were to make a loan of a comparable degree of uncertainty. The reason for its willingness to devote its retained profits to such a project, rather than obtaining a better return by lending the money to someone else, is that this sort of loan (and indeed the acquisition of financial assets in general), while it would increase the non-trading income of the firm, would add nothing to its sales revenue.† But the firm will be reluctant to

---

* See, for example, Marris (1964a), especially ch. 2, and Baumol (1967). The prominence given to sales figures in company reports is not fortuitous; nor is the fact that the *Fortune* 500 are ranked in order of sales revenue. But I do not agree with Marris that this pattern of behaviour is caused by the separation of ownership from control. Instead, I believe it to reflect the fact that (in so far as the two conflict) the urge for power is stronger than the urge for money. As a result, growth maximisation is a phenomenon which is to be observed in (all except the smallest) unincorporated firms and in closely owned companies as well as in large quoted companies with widely dispersed ownership. Incidentally, it ought also to be stressed that growth maximisation is likely to entail cost minimisation in most senses of the word; thus many of the propositions of neoclassical theory require no modification – see Baumol (1967) pp. 55–8.

† Thus the main reason why financial companies have specifically been excluded from the scope of the present theory is that their sales of goods and services are relatively insignificant, while their principal activities involve the acquisition and disposal of financial assets of various kinds. In consequence, financial companies probably do for the most part possess the type

borrow money to finance investment projects of this kind, even if the interest rate involved is no higher than that which the firm could obtain if it made a loan of what it regarded as a comparable degree of risk. For eventual bankruptcy becomes a virtual certainty if the firm borrows for the purpose of undertaking more than a few projects whose expected rate of return is less than the interest rate on the debt in question.

The net result of these various considerations is that the neoclassical picture of finance is utterly untenable as a description of the real world. Indeed, debt is in practice of comparatively minor significance as a source of finance for company investment. Although firms engage extensively in borrowing of a temporary or short run character, they are obliged to rely mainly on other sources of finance in the long run. Moreover, for reasons which also derive mainly from ignorance in the capital market (and which will be discussed at length below), firms can finance only a tiny proportion of their investment by new issues of shares. Thus the great bulk (in Britain, more than three-quarters)* of the finance for company investment is provided, and must necessarily be provided, from retained profits (including depreciation provisions). It is this that opens the door for the present theory, since it establishes a link between current investment and current profits which is absent in neoclassical theory, where current investment is related only to *future* profits.†

1.3 HISTORY OF THE THEORY

The central principle of the present theory has never formed part of the mainstream orthodoxy of economics. But closely related ideas have surfaced from time to time, and it is of some interest to trace their history and to place them in context.

of motivation which neoclassical theory erroneously attributes to all firms, namely the maximisation of the present value of future earnings.

* See, for example, *National Income and Expenditure*, 1973, Tables 28–9, and the *Annual Abstract of Statistics*, 1971, Tables 384–7.

† There may be some economists who will regard the present theory as a 'special case' of neoclassical theory. To me, this proposition seems no truer than its converse. But even if the proposition were true, it would still be necessary to recognise that the special case in question happens to be the only one of general practical relevance.

Much of the recent work in this area stems from the models developed by Downie (1958) and Steindl (1952), who was a pupil of Kalecki. But, important though their ideas were, neither of these writers achieved a major impact. There are several reasons for this. One is that both men were concerned primarily with issues other than the theory of profits – Steindl with the prospect of secular stagnation and Downie with the sources of technical progress – and their models of the determination of profits were to some extent incidental to these larger issues. Moreover, they did not make clear the nature of their departures from orthodox theory, nor did either of them undertake an adequate discussion of the financial behaviour of firms, a matter central to their models.

However, Downie's ideas in particular were picked up by a number of subsequent writers, including Marris and Ball.* But it should be noted that Marris (by contrast with Ball) has tended to avoid any attempt to develop a theory specifically of profits, even though he has made substantial contributions to other aspects of the theory of the firm.† This is not unrelated to the fact that he has moved away from his original, essentially practical, view of the financial circumstances of companies towards something more similar to what I described above as the neoclassical position.‡ Marris's opinions in this regard diverge sharply from those of Kaldor, who (more or less independently) has put forward a macroeconomic model which incorporates the central principle of the present theory. This model is contained in Kaldor's 'Neo-Pasinetti Theorem' (Kaldor, 1966, pp. 316–19). Its nature will be explored more fully below, especially in relation to Kaldor's earlier theories of the distribution of income.

But, to take a longer view, it is not too fanciful to argue that the

* Marris (1964a) and Ball (1964) pp. 109–16. Ball's model is used by Cyert and George (1969). Similar ideas may be discerned in a number of other recent growth models of the firm, most notably in Baumol (1967), and in Eichner (1973).

† An exception to this tendency being his 'Incomes Policy and the Rate of Profit in Industry' (Marris, 1964b).

‡ Specifically, Marris has attached less and less importance to his 'finance function' as such, and more and more importance to his 'valuation function'. This movement can be traced from *Managerial Capitalism* (Marris, 1964a), via *The Corporate Economy* (Marris and Wood, 1971), to 'Why Economics Needs a Theory of the Firm' (Marris, 1972).

roots of the present theory may be observed in the work of certain classical economists. The earliest of these appears to be Ricardo, who put forward the proposition that savings are made chiefly out of profits.* There are a number of ways in which this proposition may be construed, but it is by no means implausible to interpret it as meaning that investment is *financed* mainly out of profits. However, Ricardo did not use this principle as part of a theory of the determination of profits. Instead, he believed that profits were in effect exogenously determined (being the residual of output after the deduction of subsistence wages and rent), and that the level of investment was dependent in a purely passive way on the level of profits.

Marx, by contrast, used the Ricardian principle to develop a theory of the determination of profits.† The conventional view, of course, is that Marx's theory of profits is no more than a trivial adaptation of Ricardo's, profits being the residual difference between an exogenously determined level of output per man and an exogenously determined subsistence wage (Kaldor, 1956; Robinson, 1942). Support for this conventional view is easily found in the pages of *Capital*. But there is also to be found a very different model, mainly in chapter XXV of volume I, which is entitled 'The General Law of Capitalist Accumulation'.

This alternative model is very similar to the present theory. Marx abandons the assumption of a secularly constant real wage, which up to that point is founded precariously on a morally and historically determined subsistence level.‡ The real wage can then rise (although the *share* of wages may fall), but 'the rise of wages is ...confined within limits that not only leave intact the foundations of the capitalistic system, but also secure its reproduction on a progressive scale' (Marx, 1906, p. 680). That is, as in the present

---

* See, for example, his *Principles* (Ricardo, 1951) p. 347. Cf. Pasinetti (1960) and Kaldor (1956).

† This was recognised by Steindl (1952) pp. 228–43. Cf. also the work of H. J. Rustow, cited by Kaldor (1970*b*) p. 5n.

‡ Marx (1906) Vol. I, p. 190. There are various ways in which the two views of distribution in Marx may be reconciled with one another, none of which is entirely satisfactory. The best is probably to treat the conventional view as a static or short run simplification in which productivity and the real wage are taken as given, and the General Law as a dynamic explanation of the secular level of the real wage in relation to productivity.

theory, profits must be large enough to finance the accumulation of capital. The amount of profits needed for this purpose depends on the proportion of profits which capitalists accumulate, which Marx (1906, pp. 648–56) discusses under the heading of 'The Abstinence Theory', and on the rate of accumulation itself, which in turn depends primarily on the strength of the capitalistic desire for growth – 'Accumulate! Accumulate! That is Moses and the prophets!'* And, as if to reinforce his inversion of the causation of Ricardo's model, Marx (p. 679) stresses that 'the rate of accumulation is the independent not the dependent variable; the rate of wages, the dependent, not the independent variable'.

But the approach which Marx adopted in 'The General Law' disappeared in the climate of economic thought of the late nineteenth and early twentieth centuries. No trace of it can be found, for example, in Marshall's *Principles* (1949), even though Marshall was well aware of the limitations and difficulties of financing investment by borrowing (see especially pp. 260, 500). The reason for this neglect would appear to be that neoclassical economists, then as now, were more interested in allocation problems in stationary states than they were in questions of accumulation and expansion. Thus it is significant that the principles of the present theory reappeared in the work of economists such as Kalecki and Schumpeter, who were unorthodox in the particular sense of being concerned mainly with problems of investment and growth. †

Keynes is more difficult to fit into the picture. The formal model of investment behaviour in the *General Theory* (Keynes, 1936) is certainly neoclassical in character. Businessmen invest up to the point at which the marginal efficiency of capital equals the interest rate, and it is implicitly assumed that they experience no difficulty in obtaining the necessary finance.‡ But it is clear from his well-known remarks about 'animal spirits' (1936, pp. 161–2) that

---

* Marx (1906) p. 652. As this phrase suggests, Marx's view of business motivation was a great deal more realistic than that of his neoclassical detractors.

† See, for example, Kalecki (1952), especially chs. 8, 9, and 10, and Schumpeter (1939). Cf. Hahn and Matthews (1965) p. 22.

‡ However, some of the confusion in the exchange between Keynes and Robertson (in the *Economic Journal* 1937–8) entitled 'Mr. Keynes and "Finance"' arose from the fact that Keynes and Robertson tended to use the word 'finance' in two different senses, neither of which is identical with the present usage.

Keynes did not believe that the neoclassical view of business motivation was altogether satisfactory. Nor, as may be seen from his references in the *Treatise* (Keynes, 1971, p. 190) to the 'fringe of unsatisfied borrowers', did Keynes subscribe without reservation to the neoclassical view of finance (although, as we shall see, the neoclassical view is certainly more appropriate to the short run context of the *General Theory* than it is to the present analysis of the long run). Moreover, 'finance problems' are evidently at the heart of the multiplier and the concept of effective demand, for if there were a neoclassical capital market consumers' current expenditures would be very largely independent of their current incomes.* Finally, of course, Keynes would never have adopted what I described above as the 'neoclassical assumptions' about uncertainty. For he went out of his way to emphasise the significance of sheer ignorance about the future and the precarious and volatile nature of expectations.

However, it is of some importance to note that the present theory is not, despite certain apparent similarities, a 'neo-Keynesian' theory of distribution of the sort developed by Kaldor, Robinson and Pasinetti.† As is well known, the essential principle of neo-Keynesian theory is that the share of profits in national income is determined by the need to make the economy's average propensity to save equal to the ratio of investment to full employment output. A vital underlying assumption of this theory is that the propensity to save out of profits is different from the propensity to save out of other sorts of income, and thus that changes in the share of profits alter the economy's (weighted) average propensity to save.

The simplest context in which to expound the neo-Keynesian theory is that of an economy in which the rate of growth of the labour force, output per man and the capital–output ratio are all exogenously given constants. In such an economy, if full employ-

---

* As has been argued by some of the 'life cycle' theorists of the consumption function. (See especially Friedman, 1957.) See also the comments of Leijonhufvud (1969) p. 42.

† Kaldor (1956), Robinson (1956, 1964), Pasinetti (1962), together with Kahn (1959). A fuller bibliography is provided on p. 205 of Harcourt (1972). To this one should probably add Boulding (1950) ch. 14, although his theory differs in certain respects from the others mentioned. The same is true of Hahn (1972).

ment is to be maintained, the rate of growth of output must be equal to the rate of growth of the labour force. To sustain this growth rate of output, given the capital–output ratio, a particular share of investment in total output is required. And if aggregate demand is to equal aggregate supply, the economy's average propensity to save must equal this necessary ratio of investment to output. Given the values of the individual propensities to save out of profits and other income, and within certain limits, this particular average propensity to save can be achieved if the share of profits takes on a particular value.

This, in its most elementary form, is the neo-Keynesian theory of the determination of the share of profits. Its essential principles diverge from those of the present theory. Confusion between them may arise because both postulate that profits are in some sense determined by investment. But the mechanisms involved are completely different. Apart from anything else, the two theories use the word 'investment' in different senses. 'Investment' in the Keynesian sense refers to autonomous expenditure (i.e. expenditure which is independent of the current level of national income), while 'investment' in the sense appropriate to the present theory refers to capital formation by the company sector. Only in a special case are the two things the same.*

More fundamentally still, the nature of the causal link between investment and profits is not the same in the two sorts of theories. For the present theory revolves around the relationship between profits and the availability of finance, an issue which is tangential to the neo-Keynesian theory, while the neo-Keynesian theory revolves around the relationship between the share of profits and the average saving propensity, an issue which is tangential to the present theory. The distinction involved is perhaps best illustrated by examining two extreme instances. First, the present theory would work perfectly well even if the propensity to save out of profits were equal to the propensity to save out of other sorts of income, a contingency which would cause the neo-Keynesian

---

* For example, autonomous expenditure includes exports, public expenditure and autonomous private consumption expenditure as well as company sector domestic capital formation. It should also be borne in mind that 'saving' in the Keynesian sense is defined as the difference between income and induced expenditure on domestic output; in particular it includes expenditure on imports and tax payments as well as the acquisition of financial assets.

theory to collapse (since there would then be no relationship between the share of profits and the average saving propensity). Second, the neo-Keynesian theory would work perfectly well even if (as in neoclassical theory) all company investment could be financed by borrowing, a contingency which would cause the present theory to collapse (since there would then be no relationship between profits and the availability of finance).

The difference between the two sorts of theory will become clearer when the principles of the present theory have been embodied in a formal macroeconomic model which can be compared directly with the neo-Keynesian model (see pp. 117, 125 and 133 below). It may be noted in passing, though, that a further source of confusion between the two sorts of theory is the fact that Kaldor has at different points adhered to both. The move away from the neo-Keynesian theory occurred in his Neo-Pasinetti Theorem (Kaldor, 1966; see also p. 118n below), although the extent of the change in his views was not made altogether clear. But a careful inspection of the Theorem reveals that the level of profits (specifically, the level of the profit *rate*) is determined by considerations of finance, while an entirely distinct mechanism, operating through the valuation ratio, perpetuates certain aspects of the neo-Keynesian viewpoint by ensuring the equality of savings and investment at full employment.

Finally, it may be worth pointing out that the present theory has little, fundamentally, to do with what have been called the 'Cambridge controversies in capital theory',* although there are inevitably certain overlaps. The controversies in question have concerned the legitimacy (in a logical sense) of certain neoclassical theories of distribution which employ a production function whose arguments include a value aggregate of capital. But, although the present theory is to some extent a critique of neoclassical theory, two things must be emphasised. First, it is a critique of Debreu-style general equilibrium models rather than of Clark-type aggregative parables. Second, it is a critique of the appropriateness of certain assumptions rather than of the internal logic of neoclassical theory.

* For a comprehensive survey of the literature, see Harcourt (1972).

1.4 OUTLINE OF THE BOOK

The purpose of this chapter has been to give some idea of the principles which underly the present theory of profits. It is clear that the financial behaviour of companies lies at the heart of the theory. In chapter 2 we shall accordingly attempt a fairly full discussion of the ways in which companies finance their investment both in the long run and in the short run. Particular attention will be paid to the factors which determine the extent to which companies borrow, the proportion of profits which they retain and the amount of finance which they raise by new issues of shares. In the course of this investigation it will be necessary to say a good deal about the valuation of shares and the nature of the influence which the stock market exercises on company behaviour.

In chapter 3 we shall embody the principles of the theory in a simple formal model of the individual firm. We shall focus on the long run profit margin decision (in effect asking how the size of the mark-up is determined). We shall discover that the level of the profit margin and the level of investment expenditure are mutually determined. Particular attention will be paid to the way in which competition between firms affects the profit margin, and a certain amount will be said about the choice of technique in relation to the investment decision. The formal model will depend on the assumption of equilibrium but an attempt will be made to explore both the long run and the short run consequences of disequilibrium.

Making use of this model of the individual firm we shall develop in chapter 4 a macroeconomic model of the determination of the share of profits in national income. To begin with, the analysis will be restricted to the context of a closed economy with no government. Subsequently, however, we shall give a great deal of attention to the influence of the government and to international considerations. A considerable amount will be said about the incidence of taxes on profits. In chapter 5 we shall explore some of the implications of the present theory of profits for government policy.

2

THE FINANCIAL BEHAVIOUR
OF COMPANIES

The basis of the present theory is the fact that profits are an essential source of finance for company investment. Its central principle is that the amount of profits which a company plans to earn is determined by the amount of investment that it intends to undertake. Before proceeding further, it is important to note that throughout this book the word 'investment' will be used to mean 'gross physical capital formation' (i.e. investment in fixed assets and stocks). Needless to say, companies also 'invest' in the quite different sense of acquiring financial assets of various kinds; we shall not neglect this sort of activity, but we shall keep it separate from physical investment.

To impart substance to the central principle of the present theory, it is obviously necessary to be able to specify exactly what level of profits would be required to finance any given level of investment. This depends on the values of three ratios.

(1) The *gross retention ratio*; this is defined as the ratio of internal finance (retained earnings and depreciation provisions) to profits. It will be denoted by the letter r.

(2) The *external finance ratio*; this is defined as the ratio of external finance (new borrowing and share issues) to investment. It will be denoted by the letter x.

(3) The *financial asset ratio*; this is defined as the ratio of the acquisition of financial assets (cash, marketable securities, etc.) to investment. It will be denoted by the letter f.

The significance of these three ratios can be seen most easily when the relationship between profits and investment is stated in algebraic terms. Let P be the level of profits and let I be the level of investment. The company's total outlay on capital account is $(1+f)I$, this being the sum of its investment and of its acquisition of financial assets. Part of this outlay is financed from external sources; the total amount of external finance is xI. The remainder of the outlay, namely $(1+f-x) I$, must be financed internally; that is, it must be equal to the amount of internal finance, rP. Thus it follows from our definitions that

$$rP = (1+f-x) I$$

and that

$$P = \frac{(1+f-x)}{r} I.$$

Given particular values for r, x and f, this equation determines the level of profits that would be needed to finance any given level of investment.*

The gross retention ratio, the external finance ratio and the financial asset ratio are, therefore, fundamental to the present theory of profits, and the purpose of this chapter is to discuss at some length the forces which determine the values taken on by these three ratios. In the course of the discussion it will be necessary to bear in mind certain definitions and accounting relationships, and in this connection it is convenient that the three ratios correspond with three accounts commonly presented in company reports. These go by various names, but we shall call them the 'appropriation account', the 'sources of funds account' and the 'uses of funds account' respectively.

The appropriation account may be set out in its simplest form as

Profits
+ Non-Trading Income
− Interest Payments
− Taxation
− Dividends
_____
Internal Finance

where 'internal finance' is the sum of retained earnings and depreciation provisions. The account is self-explanatory and does

---

* The equation also, incidentally, emphasises in a formal way something that should be intuitively obvious, namely that for the present theory to make sense $(x-f)$ must be less than unity and r must be greater than zero. In other words, there must be some need for internal finance, and profits must generate some internal finance.

not depend on any unusual definitions.* It shows that the value of the gross retention ratio depends on the extent of non-trading income, interest payments, taxation and dividends in relation to profits.

The sources of funds account states that

> Internal Finance
> + Proceeds of New Share Issues
> + Net New Borrowing
> _____
> Total Sources of Funds

It shows that the value of the external finance ratio depends on the extent of new share issues and net new borrowing in relation to investment. The uses of funds account, in the form in which we shall consider it, states that

> Investment
> + Acquisition of Financial Assets
> _____
> Total Uses of Funds

Double entry book-keeping principles ensure that Total Uses of Funds are identically equal to Total Sources of Funds.

The discussion of the determination of the gross retention ratio, the external finance ratio and the financial asset ratio which occupies the remainder of the present chapter is in effect an item-by-item investigation of these three accounts. An attempt will be made to explain how the magnitudes of the individual elements of the accounts are determined, the intention being that the answers to these detailed enquiries shall add up to an explanation of the magnitudes of the three ratios in question. The next section of the chapter will discuss borrowing, interest payments, non-trading income and the acquisition of financial assets. Subsequent sections will deal with dividends and new share issues. We shall immediately consider the remaining items, namely depreciation provisions and taxation.

Depreciation provisions, which constitute a major proportion

* Although it is of course necessary to adopt mutually consistent definitions of the variables involved. This is particularly true of 'taxation' and 'dividends'. We shall in fact consider dividends gross and taxation net of personal income taxes, but this is by no means essential.

of internal finance, are the allowances made by a company's accountants for the wearing out and obsolescence of its fixed assets. However, although an accountant would treat these provisions as costs in the course of calculating the earnings of the firm, they do not represent current outlays. Instead, to the extent that the firm's profits are sufficient to cover these provisions, they are available for expenditure on its investment activities (which may, but need not, include projects involving the 'replacement' of fixed assets). The size of the provision for depreciation in any one year is determined by the pattern of the firm's past investment expenditures and by the depreciation rules applied by its accountants (which we shall take as given).*

The amount of taxation paid by a company depends straightforwardly on the extent of its profits and non-trading income, on the allowances made by the authorities in the calculation of taxable income, on the nature of the company tax system and on the tax rates. Allowances for tax purposes normally include interest payments and depreciation provisions (which, although calculated on similar principles, are not necessarily the same as those discussed in the preceding paragraph).† We shall take the nature of the tax system and the tax rates to be exogenously given (although we shall need to take account of the existence of a range of alternative possible company tax systems).

At this point it is convenient to say something about expenditure on mergers and the acquisition of subsidiaries. For in reality such expenditure would appear as a separate item in the uses of funds account, in addition to 'Investment' and 'Acquisition of Financial Assets'. But from the point of view of the present theory, most expenditure on mergers and the acquisition of subsidiaries is irrelevant, as are most new issues of securities made in connec-

---

* There are a variety of these rules. There is, of course, controversy in accounting circles as to which of them should be used, especially in periods of inflation. But the details of this controversy are for the most part irrelevant to the present argument, which requires only that some given set of rules should be applied. It may be noted in passing that the present theory of profits could quite easily be reworked in net of depreciation terms, although little would be gained by so doing.

† 'Accelerated depreciation' for tax purposes being an inducement to investment which is commonly offered by the government. For reasons of symmetry, we shall treat investment grants as negative tax payments.

tion with such expenditure. To explain why this is so, it is necessary to divide mergers and acquisitions into five categories.

(1) Mergers by exchange of securities: this refers to situations where, for example, company A takes over company B by making a new issue of company A shares to the shareholders of company B in exchange for their company B shares. As far as the present theory is concerned, this sort of operation is completely irrelevant. For it represents no more than an arbitrary alteration of the demarcation lines between companies. Moreover, new issues of this kind raise no additional finance for the companies involved (in the sense that they permit no increase in the sum of the capital outlays of A and B). We shall therefore ignore this type of activity altogether.

(2) Purchase of subsidiaries for cash: this refers to situations where, for example, company A purchases from company B one of its subsidiaries (company B1), for cash.* As far as the present theory is concerned, this sort of expenditure is relevant from the viewpoint of the individual companies in question, but not from the viewpoint of the company sector as a whole. The distinction is significant because our ultimate interest lies in the share of profits in national income and thus in the investment and finances of the company sector as a whole rather than of any individual company. Strictly speaking, in considering the determination of the profit margin of the individual company we should take account of the fact that the purchase and sale of subsidiaries for cash constitute respectively an additional use and an additional source of funds. But the net total of such purchases and sales within the company sector is necessarily zero. For simplicity, therefore, we shall neglect them even at the level of the individual company.†

---

* We shall define 'subsidiary' to mean 'consolidated subsidiary'. (A consolidated subsidiary need not be wholly owned by the parent company, but we shall neglect the complications introduced by minority interests.) All other interests of one company in the equity of another will be classified as financial assets. ('Financial assets' is thus a term which covers 'trade investments' and 'investments in unconsolidated subsidiaries' as well as 'investments' in the usual sense.) Incidentally, the present comments on the purchase and sale of subsidiaries apply directly also to the purchase and sale of second-hand physical assets (other than those which form part of going concerns).

† Although their introduction into the microeconomic model in chapter 3 would not give rise to any problem of principle.

(3) Purchase of subsidiaries for securities: this refers to situations where, for example, company A purchases from company B one of its subsidiaries (company B2), the consideration received by company B taking the form of a new issue of company A shares (worth, say, £1 million). This sort of activity is relevant to the present theory, even from the point of view of the company sector as a whole. For although the net value of such purchases and sales of subsidiaries within the company sector is necessarily zero, the new issues of securities involved do raise additional finance for the company sector.* (The reason for this is that the new issue enables company A to increase its total capital expenditure by £1 million, while company B's total capital expenditure is unaffected by the transaction, since it can, for example, sell the new company A shares on the open market and use the proceeds to finance its investment. Hence the sum of the sources of funds of A and B is increased by £1 million.) Thus, while we shall omit the actual purchases and sales of such subsidiaries from our analysis (since they cancel out for the company sector as a whole), we must include new issues of this kind in the sources of funds account.

(4) Mergers involving a cash consideration: this refers to situations in which, for example, company A takes over company B by purchasing the shares of company B from the shareholders of company B for cash (the total payment being, say, £2 million). This type of merger (unlike the mergers in category 1) is relevant to the present theory, even though it represents no more than an arbitrary change in the demarcation lines between companies. For the cash purchase of the shares of company B by company A is tantamount to a negative new issue. That is, as a result of the operation, the sum of the capital expenditures of A and B must be £2 million less than it would otherwise have been. Thus although we shall exclude expenditure on such mergers from the uses of funds account, we must subtract such repurchases of securities from the relevant items in the sources of funds account.

---

* Thus the official statisticians are wrong in treating such issues as 'no new money' issues and in excluding them from the series which appears, for example, in the *Annual Abstract of Statistics* (Table 367 in the 1971 edn). The way in which this official series is constructed is explained in the *Bank of England Quarterly Bulletin*, June 1966.

(5) Acquisition of unincorporated businesses: this refers to situations in which, for example, company A buys, as a going concern, an unincorporated business, either for cash or by making a new issue of company A shares to its owner. This sort of activity is relevant to the present theory, since it involves a net acquisition of assets by the company sector (of a type which can be subsumed under neither of the two existing headings in the uses of funds account). Moreover, if a new issue of securities is involved, this represents an addition to the sources of funds of the company sector. No problem of principle would be caused by the inclusion of such transactions in the uses and sources of funds accounts, but it would make the accounts somewhat more complicated. There-fore, since this type of expenditure is very small in relation to the magnitude of the other variables with which we shall be dealing, we shall ignore it completely.*

Finally, it is perhaps worth commenting on the fact that much of the discussion of financial behaviour below relates specifically to quoted companies, those, that is, whose securities are quoted on a stock exchange. Such companies do in fact constitute the core of the company sector.† However, the principles of the argument apply also, *mutatis mutandis*, to unquoted companies. There are of course a number of significant differences between the two types of companies. One is that new issues of shares to the public are a source of finance which is confined to quoted companies, although additional shares in unquoted companies can in some cases be sold privately. Another is that the interests of the shareholders of an unquoted company cannot normally be framed in terms of the market value of their shares. A third is that the ownership of unquoted companies is normally less diffuse and this (together with the fact that shareholders cannot readily sell their shares) causes a closer integration of ownership and control which may have implications, for example, for dividend policy. However,

---

* Incidentally, the incorporation of existing unincorporated businesses is of no relevance from a purely financial point of view (since it amounts to no more than an arbitrary change in the position of the demarcation line between the company sector and the unincorporated business sector). But see pp. 140–1 below.

† At present, in the U.K., they account for about three-quarters of gross company profits. See *National Income and Expenditure*, 1971, Table 1 and *Annual Abstract of Statistics*, 1972, Table 396.

from the point of view of the present theory, the behaviour of unquoted companies is likely, broadly speaking, to be fundamentally the same as that of quoted companies.

2.2 BORROWING AND FINANCE IN THE LONG RUN AND THE SHORT RUN

In the course of developing the present theory of profits we shall make considerable use of the terms 'long run' and 'short run'. It is therefore necessary to attempt an immediate explanation of the sense in which these terms are used, although the distinction in question will become clearer as the exposition proceeds. By 'long run' decisions we mean what others have called 'strategic' decisions, being those decisions which exercise a fundamental influence on the firm's behaviour over a period of, say, three to five years.* These are to be contrasted with 'short run' (or 'operating') decisions, which control the firm's activities from month to month or year to year.

It is important to recognise that this distinction is more than an arbitrary difference of time period. It is, rather, a distinction between two different business states of mind. For it is central to the present argument that businessmen have long run views of the development of their companies within which they make strategic decisions which establish certain long run targets. This is not to deny that the great bulk of business decisions are concerned with the short run. But short run decisions are made in the context of, and are strongly influenced by, the long run targets of the company.

The present theory relates to the long run. In particular, the proposition that the amount of profits which a company plans to earn is determined by the amount of investment which it intends to undertake is a proposition which is true only in the long run.† This is so partly because most investment decisions, being concerned with the installation of capacity, are subject to substantial gestation periods. Thus to some extent 'short run' decisions are

---

* Cf. Ansoff (1965) and Lintner (1971), especially pp. 172–6 and the references cited on p. 174.
† Thus when we spoke on p. 9 above of a link between current profits and current investment, we were using the word 'current' in the somewhat unusual sense of 'in the long run'.

simply those which are made with reference to time periods over which, for purely technical reasons, the level of the firm's capacity cannot be varied (although the degree to which it is used can vary). 'Long run' decisions, by contrast, are those which are made with reference to a time horizon sufficiently distant that the level of capacity is a variable within the firm's control. But the distinction between the long run and the short run involves something more than whether or not the level of capacity can be varied. For it also reflects the fact that in making price and output decisions businessmen think (and must inevitably think) in terms of relatively predictable long run trends in demand around which the level of demand fluctuates in the short run in ways that are more or less impossible to predict. That is, the firm must adopt policies which are 'long run' also in the sense that they relate to trends over, say, a three to five year period ahead. In consequence, the firm's profit-making intentions (expressed in its target profit margin and target output levels) are an integral part of what is necessarily a long run sales strategy.

It follows from this that the discussion in the present chapter must be directed mainly towards long run or strategic financial behaviour. That is, the principal object of the chapter is to explain what determines the long run target values of the gross retention ratio, the external finance ratio and the financial asset ratio. These financial targets will be seen to depend in turn on certain underlying targets which are the outcome of strategic decisions with regard to such things as the firm's dividend policy and the proportion of debt in its capital structure.

But the firm must also have a short run financial policy. For even if its long run planning is successful in the sense that, over a four year period, its gross retained profits finance the planned proportion of its investment outlays, it is most unlikely that retained profits and internal finance requirements will move in line with one another from month to month or from year to year. There are two reasons for this. One is that it would be costly and inconvenient for the firm to have to tailor its investment to its profits in the short run, even if it could foresee the future with great precision. The other is that the firm in fact cannot accurately predict the time pattern of its receipts and expenditures. As a result, the amount of internal finance generated in any short period may exceed or fall short of planned (internally financed) investment outlays, and the firm must have a flexible short run financial policy to cope with both the expected and the unexpected discrepancies. Short run finance policies contain two main elements.

The first is the acquisition and disposal of financial assets. For any excess of receipts on capital account over planned expenditures can be absorbed by the acquisition of financial assets. Even more important, temporary excesses of planned expenditures over receipts can be financed by the disposal of financial assets; in such cases, the company simply alters the form in which it holds its assets, for example by transforming a thousand pounds worth of government securities into a thousand pounds worth of plant and machinery. This is a procedure which has great advantages for the company. For to the extent that it has a reserve of financial assets, its capacity installation programme can be independent both of short run vagaries of demand and profits and of the availability of short term credit facilities.

Thus all companies aim to operate with a 'liquidity cushion' of financial assets (see Kaldor, 1966, p. 314). That is, as part of its long run financial strategy, the company will plan to hold, on average, a certain minimum proportion of its assets in liquid form. Moreover, for reasons that will become more apparent later, the desire of those in charge of the company to expand its sales will ensure that in the long run its financial asset holdings do not exceed this necessary minimum. The exact level of the long run minimum (or target) ratio of financial to physical assets will vary among companies according to their circumstances. It will depend primarily on (a) the expected size and duration of future short run deficits on capital account, (b) the expected availability of short term credit facilities and (c) the extent of the losses which would be incurred by the interruption or postponement of planned investment expenditures.* In the short run, of course, the firm's financial asset holdings will fluctuate around their long run target level in response to temporary deficits and surpluses on capital account.

From this it can be seen that the long run target value of the

* It will also be influenced to some degree by the rate of return on financial assets and by the advantages to be gained by acquiring a measure of control over the activities of other companies (see p. 21n above).

financial asset ratio is determined by the desire of the firm to maintain a particular level of financial working capital in relation to the extent of its physical capital. In the short run, however, the actual financial asset ratio will vary (both in size and in sign) around the long run target. Likewise, the extent of the firm's non-trading income is determined in the long run by the firm's liquidity target and by the rate of return on financial assets, but is subject to short run fluctuations around its long run trend.

The second main element of short run finance policies is of course short term borrowing, principally from banks and similar financial institutions.* Short term lending is, indeed, the most important service which banks perform for industrial and commercial companies. For (at least in the U.K.) banks have traditionally been reluctant to engage in long term lending, but have thrived instead on the provision of two sorts of bridging credit. The first is loans to finance working capital (stocks and work in progress). The second is loans to provide short run (or temporary) finance for fixed investment projects. For example, a company might wish to borrow temporarily from the banks to finance the initial stages of the construction of a new factory, even though, over a two year period, it intended to repay the loan and finance the expenditure entirely out of retained profits. Similarly, a company might obtain a temporary loan from a bank if, in the course of building a factory, it found its cash flow over some three month period to be less than it had anticipated. Thus the behaviour of short term borrowing is similar to that of financial asset holdings. In the long run an expanding company will expect to incur, on average, an increasing amount of short term debt, both because it will require an increasing amount of working capital and because it will be engaged in an increasing number of fixed investment projects. In any short period, however, its net new short term borrowing may be either positive or negative, depending on the sign and size of temporary discrepancies on capital account.

* Strictly speaking, we ought also to include trade credit (as borrowing and lending between firms is called) as an additional source of short term borrowing. But trade credit very largely cancels out, both for individual companies and for the company sector as a whole, since all companies both buy and sell on credit to some extent. In the long run, net trade credit given or received may be added to or subtracted from the required level of financial working capital.

2-2

The availability and cost of short term credit from the banks varies over time (largely in response to governmental pressure). It also varies among companies, according to their size, the riskiness of their activities, the 'realisability' of their assets and the extent of their outstanding debts. This may mean, among other things, that the *length* of the 'long run' varies among companies to some extent. For the greater reluctance of the banks to provide bridging credit may well force a small and risky firm to confine its strategic planning to a time horizon which is shorter than that of a large and well-established firm. Thus the distinction between the long run and the short run which, as a difference of kind, is common to all companies, may be seen also as a difference of degree which varies from company to company.

At this point it is appropriate to adjourn the discussion of short run finance policy and to return to the subject of long run behaviour. For borrowing is also an essential part of a company's long run financial strategy, although in a strategic context short term bank credit is of less importance than long term borrowing in the form of debentures or loan stock.* (In the long run the share of bank credit in a company's total debt will depend primarily on its ratio of working to fixed capital.) Let us therefore examine the factors which determine the extent to which companies borrow in the long run (without regard to short run fluctuations in the level of borrowing around the long run trend, which occur for reasons that have already been mentioned).† Of particular importance in this respect are the various sorts of risks and disadvantages entailed by lending and borrowing, all of which derive in one way or another from uncertainty and ignorance about the future course of the company's profits. We shall accordingly consider these risks and disadvantages in some detail.

Lenders' risk is very straightforward. It is the risk that, in the event of the company going bankrupt, lenders will not get their principal back because the saleable assets of the company are insufficient to cover its liabilities. Lenders' risk makes itself felt initially in the need for the company to offer some sort of security

* For simplicity we shall regard preference shares as a type of loan stock.
† On the subject of borrowing, see for example, Marris (1964a) pp. 7–9, Kalecki (1952) ch. 8, Kaldor (1970a), and Marshall (1949) pp. 259–60 and 500. See also the discussion on pp. 4–9 above.

in order to be able to borrow. It also means that, to attract loans, a company must pay a higher interest rate the higher its gearing ratio (which we shall define as the ratio of total outstanding debt to the current realisable value of total assets – the latter approximating fairly closely to the current replacement cost of total assets less depreciation).* Eventually, too high a gearing ratio will lead to outright refusals to lend at any interest rate.

Borrowers' risk is slightly more complicated. It is ultimately the risk that the company might be forced into bankruptcy as a result of an unforeseen fall in profits so great that it could no longer meet its fixed interest obligations. Even before this stage there is the risk that a somewhat smaller fall in profits might cause effective control over the company to pass into the hands of its creditors, who might insist on the resignation or dismissal of those who were previously in charge of the company. Added to which there is the risk that, when loans mature, lenders might refuse to renew them (or might agree to renew them only at an unacceptably high rate of interest) and thus the company might be obliged to sell off part of its assets to repay a loan, a contingency which could easily result in the closure of the company.

Moreover, there is the further disadvantage to extensive borrowing that a high gearing ratio (together with relatively stable dividends) amplifies the proportional effect of short run fluctuations of profits on the short run level of retained profits. This greater variability of retained profits makes it desirable to have better temporary credit facilities available. However, a high gearing ratio makes banks more reluctant to provide additional short term credit, because of the greater burden of outstanding debt. One consequence of this is that the firm must maintain larger holdings of financial assets if it is to be able to implement its long run investment strategy in the face of short run variations in demand. Another, more serious, consequence is that the firm is more vulnerable to the sort of collapse which is caused by a chain reaction of refusals to lend based on the self-justifying expectation

* The distinction between the current realisable value of assets and their historical cost is very important in periods in which the rate of change of prices is significant. For inflation causes the money value of physical assets to increase, while the money value of debt remains constant. This influences the willingness of companies to borrow; see p. 32n below.

of a company's imminent demise. For companies which are heavily dependent on borrowed money commonly fall victims to sudden changes in the confidence of lenders about their future credit-worthiness.

The risks and disadvantages of borrowing affect both the owners of a company and its managers and other employees. The owners are affected in two ways. First, the higher a company's gearing ratio, the more volatile and uncertain are its earnings (which are in effect the income of its owners). Secondly, the owners risk the loss of their capital in the event of the company going bankrupt, because the break-up value of the assets of a company is usually substantially less than its value as a going concern. The managers of a company (who may also be among its owners), together with its other employees, are running a different sort of risk, namely that in the event of bankruptcy or other serious financial difficulties they may lose their jobs, which may in turn ruin their careers. In cases where the owners are shareholders in a quoted company, they can reduce their risks by spreading their shareholdings among different companies. This course of action, however, is not often open to the owners of unquoted companies. Nor, of course, is it open to managers and other employees, whose commitment to a particular company is normally total.

Risks and disadvantages of these various kinds set a limit to the amounts that companies borrow. In the long run, borrowers' risk (and especially risk to managers and to the owners of unquoted companies) is a tighter constraint than lenders' risk, for two reasons. (1) One is that lenders, like the shareholders of a quoted company, need not commit themselves to a particular company; they can spread their risks so that the insolvency of one company would not mean personal ruin. But managers and the owners of unquoted companies cannot spread their risks; their personal careers and fortunes are at stake. (2) The second reason is that it requires a much less serious crisis to inflict damage on borrowers than on lenders. For the lender is secure as long as the sale of the company's assets would suffice to discharge its liabilities. But even if a company is solvent in this ultimate sense, its managers and owners can be afflicted (as has been explained above) by a whole catalogue of losses of a type peculiar to borrowers.

In the long run, therefore, companies will normally be more

cautious about borrowing than lenders about lending. (In the short run, however, the reverse may be the case; that is, companies would often like to borrow more from banks to tide themselves over cash flow problems than banks are prepared to lend. Indeed, it is the fear of such refusals that causes a company to want a cushion of liquid assets.) More precisely, it follows from the considerations discussed above that borrowers' risk will set some upper limit on the company's long run gearing ratio. Moreover, for reasons which will be explained more fully in the next chapter, the company's desire to grow as rapidly as possible will ensure that in the long run it borrows up to this gearing limit.

The exact level of the gearing limit depends on two sorts of things. (1) Managerial expectations of the future course of the company's profits, with special reference to the chances of the company's profitability falling to very low levels (or, more precisely, with special reference to the lower tails of the subjective probability distributions of the company's profit rate in future periods). These expectations, in conjunction with expectations about the level of the interest rate (which will increase with the gearing ratio, but which in other respects we will treat as given), determine the subjective probabilities of bankruptcy and of financial difficulties of a lesser kind at each level of the gearing ratio.* (2) Which level of the gearing ratio is chosen as a limit and as a target will then depend on the attitudes of managers and owners towards the risks and disadvantages of borrowing, and in particular on the degree to which they are risk averse.

The gearing limit chosen by a firm may alter over time (for example in response to secular changes in the rate of interest). In practice, however, firms tend to adhere to particular gearing ratios for long periods. The average gearing ratio of industrial and commercial companies in the U.K. (and in the U.S.) is about 20 per cent, although there is considerable variation among companies. In particular, for the reasons explained in the previous

---

* In this regard, it should be stressed, it is the *money* rate of interest that is relevant. For the degree of risk attached to any particular level of the gearing ratio depends on the ratio of interest payments to profits, which is by definition equal to $x'u/\rho$, where x' is the gearing ratio, ρ is the profit rate (the ratio of profits to total assets) and u is the money rate of interest. However, as we shall see (p. 32n), the external finance ratio, as distinct from the gearing ratio, depends on the *real* rate of interest.

paragraph, the more volatile a firm's profits, the lower will be its chosen gearing limit. For instance, firms in capital goods industries, which are subject to greater cyclical fluctuations, tend to be less geared than firms in consumer goods industries.*

In the long run, then, the amount of external finance which a company raises by borrowing is determined by its chosen gearing ratio and by the extent of the growth in the value of its total assets, which in turn depends on (a) the amount of investment it undertakes, (b) its acquisition of financial assets, (c) the depreciation of its assets through wearing out and obsolescence and (d) any appreciation in the value of its existing assets as a result of inflation (or, more specifically, as a result of increases in the prices of the types of asset in question).† In the short run, however, the firm's borrowing will fluctuate around the long run trend in response to temporary deficits and surpluses on capital account. Correspondingly, although the long run trend of a company's interest payments depends on its long run borrowing strategy (and on the average rate of interest payable on its debt), the level of interest payments will fluctuate in the short run around the long run trend.

2.3 THE INTERESTS OF ORDINARY SHAREHOLDERS

In the last two sections of this chapter we shall consider dividend policy and new issues of shares, aspects of financial behaviour which are particularly closely bound up with the interests of ordinary shareholders. We shall begin, however, with a more general discussion of the interests of shareholders, with particular reference to the way in which they depend on company behaviour and influence company decisions.

The sole interest of the shareholder, we may reasonably assume,

---

* For some evidence on gearing behaviour in time series and cross-section, see Marris (1971), Gordon (1962), and Singh and Whittington (1968) pp. 45–7.

† Thus although, as we explained above (p. 31n), the gearing ratio depends only on the *money* interest rate, the extent of new borrowing in any long period is influenced also by the rate of inflation of prices. For this raises the value of the firm's existing assets, which, given a particular gearing ratio, increases the proportion of investment that can be financed by new borrowing. In this way, the external finance ratio in effect depends on the *real* interest rate.

THE FINANCIAL BEHAVIOUR OF COMPANIES

lies in earning the highest possible rate of return on his shares (making due allowance for risk). Equally straightforwardly, the rate of return on a share over a given period depends on three things: (a) the price of the share at the beginning of the period, (b) the amount of dividends received during the period (net of tax) and (c) the extent of the capital gain or loss resulting from any change in the price of the share over the period (net of tax and transactions costs). Matters become more complicated, however, when we turn to investigate the impact of a company's behaviour on the rate of return earned by its shareholders.

The complications in question arise from the fact that the rate of return on a share depends only in part on the behaviour of the company concerned. It depends also, of course, on the behaviour of the stock market. Specifically, the company has direct control over only one of the three things which govern the rate of return, namely the amount of dividends, while it is the stock market which directly determines the other two, namely the initial share price and the extent to which the share price rises or falls. Naturally, the company's actions will have an effect on its share price, since they will affect the market's expectations of its future dividends and earnings. But this channel of influence is necessarily of a somewhat indirect kind. Moreover, the price of any share will depend to some extent purely on the stock market's current expectations of its own future expectations.

Although in general the rate of return on a share depends both on the behaviour of the company and on the behaviour of the stock market, there are two limiting cases of considerable interest. One concerns unquoted companies in whose shares there is no market; given the cost of the original stake in such a company, the rate of return earned by its shareholders must depend solely on the behaviour of the company with regard to the payment of dividends. The other limiting case, in which the behaviour of the company has *no* effect on the rate of return earned by its shareholders, is that of equilibrium in a perfect stock market under certainty.*

* We shall assume in what follows that the absolute rate of return prevailing in the stock market is exogenously determined, for example by the actions of the government with regard to the interest rate. Even if this assumption is not made, the argument below retains its validity for the individual share-

The latter case, despite the artificiality of its assumptions, deserves further attention. It arises very simply, (a) from the equilibrium condition that, ex ante, all shares should offer the same rate of return, and (b) from the assumption of certainty, which ensures that ex post rates of return are equal to ex ante rates of return. In such circumstances, no matter how well or how badly any company is expected to perform in terms of dividends and earnings, its share price will adjust until its shares offer the same rate of return as all other shares. A 'bad' company will have a low share price, and a 'good' company will have a high share price, but shareholders will be indifferent between them.

What is remarkable about this result, incidentally, is not the result itself, but the fact that most of the economists who have put forward equilibrium models of the stock market under certainty have also tended to take it for granted that the welfare of a company's shareholders is reflected in the level of its share price. This is curious because, as we have seen, under these assumptions about the stock market, a shareholder is no better off if he buys the shares of a 'valuation–maximising' company than he would be if he bought the shares of a company that took no notice of its share price.

Moreover, this result, which was derived above under highly unrealistic assumptions about the stock market, remains of some relevance even when the assumptions are relaxed. Consider, for example, a world in which, although the future is uncertain, shareholders all have the same expectations (and, for simplicity, the same utility functions). In equilibrium, ex ante, all shares will again offer the same rate of return (adjusted for risk), and shareholders will again be indifferent as to which shares they buy (even though they know that, ex post, different shares will exhibit different rates of return). Consequently, as in the case above, the expected behaviour of individual companies will have no effect on the (risk-adjusted) rate of return expected by their shareholders.

Ex post, of course, the behaviour of individual companies will have made a difference to the rates of return earned by their shareholders, but only in a peculiarly indirect way. For an above-average rate of return will be realised in cases where a company has exceeded the prior expectations of the stock market, and a

holder, even though it ceases to be strictly valid for the collectivity of all shareholders in all companies.

34

below-average rate in cases where a company has failed to live up to the market's prior expectations. It must immediately be added that this has nothing to do with the absolute goodness or badness of a company's performance with regard to dividends and earnings. For a company whose performance in these respects was excellent by comparison with other companies might have been over-rated in advance by the stock market, while a company with a miserable record might nonetheless have exceeded the even more pessimistic expectations of the stock market.

In reality, matters are made a good deal more complicated by the fact that expectations about the returns from holding any given share vary widely among different shareholders. Ex ante, there will be disagreement both as to which companies are 'good' and which are 'bad' and as to how the stock market will react to a company's future performance. Some investors will favour the prospects of one share, while others will favour the prospects of another share. Thus at any particular set of share prices, different shares will appear to any one investor to offer different rates of return, and any one share will appear to different investors to offer different rates of return.*

In these circumstances, ex ante, it clearly matters to the shareholder which shares he buys. The golden rule is very simple, being to buy those shares which the market has undervalued and to avoid those shares which the market has overvalued (over and under-valuation referring to the current price of the share in relation to the returns expected by the individual). Equally simply, the art of making money in these circumstances lies in having more accurate expectations than the mass of shareholders. Once again, ex post, the behaviour of a company will have affected the rate of return earned by its shareholders, but again in an indirect way. For the companies whose shares yield the best rates of return will

* For the moment we shall neglect the fact that different shareholders, as well as holding different expectations, are also differently situated with regard to their utility functions, tax positions, and so on. Moreover, the concept of stock market equilibrium where expectations differ is rather complicated, and must involve limits on the investible resources of individual shareholders established by limits either on their wealth or on their borrowing power. In this connection, one would also like to say more about portfolio selection behaviour, especially with regard to diversification in the face of risk.

be those which live up to the expectations of their particular share-holder clienteles and confound the expectations of the stock market at large. Correspondingly, shareholders will suffer poor rates of return in cases in which they were over-optimistic either about the performance of their pet companies or about the reaction of the stock market to that performance.

This in itself could be said to have certain limited implications for the way in which companies ought to behave towards their shareholders. For it might be argued that although a company cannot ensure an above-average rate of return for its shareholders, it should try to preserve them from a poor rate of return by making clear in advance its own expectations and intentions with regard to future prospects and then endeavouring to live up to them. In this vein, companies sometimes make announcements designed to promote 'orderly dealing' in their shares and in particular to prevent what they regard as unjustified movements of individual share prices. But such interventions are rare, and unsurprisingly are not always effective when they occur.

The general conclusion to which one is drawn, then, seems to be that the behaviour of a company has only the most limited and indirect influence on the welfare of its shareholders. For the rate of return which they earn appears to depend on the company's performance only in relation to sets of expectations (including expectations of expectations) over whose formation the company exercises little control. The dominant influence on shareholder welfare would appear instead to be the behaviour, and particularly the speculative behaviour, of the stock market.

However, we have not by any means arrived at the end of the story. For so far we have entirely overlooked the question of the *period* for which a share is held. Throughout the preceding dis-cussion we have assumed, in effect, that most shareholders con-tinually contemplate altering their portfolios in the light of current share prices and their current expectations of future prospects. Indeed, it is this propensity to mobility which causes the interests of shareholders to become removed from the behaviour of companies. For, to the extent that the world is certain, it is mobility that causes the rates of return on all shares to tend to equality, and, to the extent that the world is uncertain, it is mobility that facilitates speculative dealing based on attempts to outguess other investors as to the future of company behaviour and stock market expectations. But such evidence as there is confutes the proposition that shareholders are a mobile population.* Both in the United Kingdom and in the United States, it would appear that the average period for which ordinary shares are held is between five and ten years, and that a significant proportion of shares are held for even longer periods.

A possible explanation of the length of the average holding period would be that share prices and expectations move in such a way as to fulfil the original expectations of most shareholders. But this cannot be taken very seriously; even within a five year period, share prices and expectations fluctuate to such an extent that it would be transparent folly for any shareholder who anticipated the timing of these fluctuations not to alter his portfolio extensively at frequent intervals, even given the existence of significant transactions costs. Transactions costs, however, are undoubtedly a part of the explanation of long holding periods, as are pure inertia and irrationality. But the principal reason for long holding periods is ignorance about the future course of both company and stock market behaviour. To begin with, investors cannot predict in any reliable way either the long term performance of individual companies or the long term reactions of the stock market. This is compounded by the fact that the speculative activities of a minority of shareholders cause substantial short term changes in share prices which are virtually unpredictable by the great majority of investors.

In consequence, the 'clientele' phenomenon acquires a temporal as well as a spatial dimension. That is, not only do particular shareholders favour particular companies at a moment of time, but they persist in their favours over considerable periods, sticking to particular shares through thick and thin. This is not, of course, true of all shareholders, but it is true of the majority, whom we may label 'long term' shareholders. They adhere to their shares in the hope of a favourable long term trend of dividends and capital gains, without regard to short term fluctuations, which they ignore because they cannot predict, and without contemplating frequent changes to the shares of other companies,

* For the U.S., see Nerlove (1968) pp. 4–6, and, for the U.K., see Revell and Moyle (1966) pp. 31–5.

about whose prospects, comparatively speaking, they are even more ignorant.

Thus, because of ignorance and uncertainty, the owners of quoted companies are led into a position which is not dissimilar to that of the owners of unquoted companies. Long term shareholders are obviously not bound to their companies for life (as Keynes once suggested all shareholders should be), but nor are they an itinerant band of speculators. As a result, their welfare depends in a much more direct way on the behaviour of the companies whose shares they own. For as long as a shareholder holds a particular share, he is directly affected by the performance of the company in question, especially with regard to dividends and retained earnings.

Retained earnings are relevant because, although a company's valuation ratio* fluctuates considerably in the short term, over the long term the growth of assets per share is the primary (and certainly the most reliable) source of capital gains. Naturally, the long term shareholder will endeavour to buy his shares at a low point of the short term cycle and to sell them at a high point, but the longer the holding period (in relation to the magnitude of the short term cycle) the smaller will be the quantitative significance of the timing of purchases and sales. The long term shareholder will, of course, be affected by any long term changes in the level of a company's valuation ratio, but in this respect also he will expect to benefit from a good performance in terms of dividends and assets per share growth. The level of a company's valuation ratio will also be subject to changes in stock market expectations about its prospects which are independent of its current performance. But such changes are on the one hand almost impossible to predict and on the other hand are likely on average (over a portfolio of different shares) to have a relatively minor impact on the extent of capital gains where long holding periods are concerned.

At the same time there exists another population of shareholders, namely short term or speculative shareholders. And it is to this population that the argument advanced in the earlier part of this section is directly applicable. For such shareholders aim to make

* The ratio of the stock market value of the ordinary shares of the company to the book value of its equity assets. The term is due to Marris (1964a).

money principally by out-guessing the stock market in the short term, and thus their welfare depends only at several removes on company behaviour. As a result, companies are for the most part indifferent to the interests of such shareholders. In other words, to the extent that the behaviour of companies (by which we must mean the behaviour of managers) is influenced by the interests of shareholders, it will be influenced by the interests specifically of long term shareholders.

It remains to enquire how, if at all, such an influence might be exercised (especially since the General Meeting can probably be ruled out as an effective vehicle for the promotion of shareholder interests). One important mechanism is that managers feel a direct moral obligation towards their long term shareholders. Another is that quite commonly managers are themselves also substantial long term shareholders, whether through stock option schemes or otherwise (see, for example, Marris, 1964a, pp. 66–78, and Lewellen, 1968). A third factor is that managers may fear the takeover of their firms if their share prices fall too low.* Even in combination, these three factors do not confer absolute power on shareholders, in the sense that in practice they are not sufficient to ensure that a company is run solely in the interests of its owners. (Indeed, if they were, there would be little basis for the present assumption that companies pursue maximum sales growth rather than maximum earnings.) Nonetheless, these factors are powerful enough to make the interests of long term shareholders the major influence on managerial decisions in certain areas, the most important of which are dividend policy and new issue policy.

In addition, it should be noted that the interests of managers are to a considerable extent the same as those of long term share-holders. This point will be elaborated at a later stage. But for the time being we may simply state that both parties have a very strong interest in the profitability of the company. From the managerial point of view, high profitability provides the means to a rapid rate of expansion. From the long term shareholder's point of view, high profitability provides the means to high dividends

---

* This hypothesis is put forward by Marris (1964a) chs. 1 and 2. The empirical investigations of Singh (1971), however, would appear to suggest that the level of a company's share price has only a rather limited effect on the probability of takeover.

and a high rate of growth of assets per share, and may also be expected to have a favourable effect on the level of the company's valuation ratio. There are of course also certain conflicts of interest between managers and long term shareholders, but these are of a secondary order of importance when compared with the extent of the community of interest between the two groups.

2.4 DIVIDEND POLICY

Thus far, in discussing the determination of the gross retention ratio, we have examined four out of its five constituent elements, namely depreciation provisions, taxation, non-trading income and interest payments. It remains to investigate the factors which determine the amount of profits paid out to ordinary shareholders in the form of dividends. In this connection we shall focus on the considerations which govern the level of a company's long run target payout ratio (the ratio of dividends to dividends plus retained earnings), although we shall also say something about short run fluctuations of the payout ratio around its long run target.

In analysing dividend policy we shall assume provisionally that there are no new issues of ordinary shares. This is not, in an empirical sense, an unreasonable assumption. In the final section of this chapter, we shall investigate the consequences of its relaxation. We shall discover that these do not materially affect our conclusions on dividend policy.

It is convenient to begin with an exposition of the neoclassical view of dividend policy (see, for example, Modigliani and Miller, 1961, 1967). Given our assumption about new issues, a neoclassical economist would regard retained earnings rather than dividends as the primary decision variable, and would regard the decision in question simply as an investment decision. The rule that management should apply in order to maximise the welfare of shareholders is in principle straightforward, being to retain earnings (i.e. invest)* up to the point where the expected rate of return (adjusted for uncertainty) on the marginal investment outlay is equal to the best expected rate of return (adjusted for uncertainty) that shareholders could obtain at the margin were

* Either in physical or in financial assets.

they to invest these funds outside the firm.* In the simplest case of equilibrium under certainty in a perfect capital market with no taxes or transactions costs, the rule would be to retain earnings up to the point at which the rate of return on the marginal investment outlay was equal to the ruling interest rate. Once the retention decision has been made in this way, management distributes the remainder of current earnings in the form of dividends.

The neoclassical approach to dividend policy has been extended to accommodate a number of complications and qualifications, such as taxation, and some account has been taken of uncertainty and of the fact that in practice shareholders are faced with a range of alternative investment opportunities of various sorts.† But the essence of the neoclassical position remains unaltered: the primary decision concerns retained earnings; an external standard of profitability (which serves as a cut-off point) is applied to the firm's investment opportunities to determine the amount of retained earnings; and dividends as such are an inconsequential residual.

However, the neoclassical position, though seductively simple and logical, is strikingly inaccurate as a description of dividend policy in the real world. For inspection of the behaviour of companies and shareholders reveals that dividends, not retained earnings, are the primary decision variable; that firms do not in general make their dividend (or investment) decisions by applying an external standard of profitability to their investment opportunities; and that dividends as such are a matter of considerable importance to shareholders. These conclusions about the nature of dividend policy in reality are supported by a substantial body of evidence, which includes detailed studies of decision making within individual companies, econometric studies of large samples of companies (considered both individually and in aggregate), and studies of the determination of share prices.‡ It is therefore

---

* For simplicity we shall ignore cases in which this rule would imply a payout ratio which was either negative or greater than unity.

† See Modigliani and Miller (1967) and, on taxation, King (1974b).

‡ For example, Lintner (1956), Kuh (1963), Meyer and Kuh (1959) – and the studies cited therein, Brittain (1964, 1966), Turnovsky (1967) and the studies cited by Friend and Puckett (1964). Friend and Puckett, incidentally, make an unsuccessful though determined attempt to pour cold water of an econometric kind on the share pricing studies in question.

of some interest to examine the neoclassical view more closely, to draw attention to those features of reality which have been over-looked by neoclassical economists, and to explain how these features cause dividend policy in practice to differ radically from the neoclassical model.

The neoclassical view of dividend policy rests on a number of self-supporting assumptions. The most fundamental of these is that shareholders can freely 'declare their own dividends' by buying or selling shares, regardless of what dividend policy is adopted by the company. This both rests upon and supports a further assumption, which is that (in the absence of certain complications introduced by taxation) the retention of $£x$ of earnings by a company will automatically be reflected in an increase of at least $£x$ in the market value of its shares. If this were the case, and if buying and selling shares were costless, neoclassical economists would un-doubtedly be correct in their assumption that shareholders are indifferent about dividends as such and care only about the level of earnings and about the investment policy of the company. For were a shareholder at any time to desire more cash (either for consumption or for investment elsewhere) than was distributed as dividends, he could readily realise some of the company's retained profits by selling some of his shares. Conversely, were a share-holder to require less cash than was distributed as dividends, he could, if he wished, simply increase his stake in the company by buying some more of its shares.

In reality, however, shareholders cannot freely declare their own dividends, and thus they are not indifferent about dividends as such. There are several important reasons for this. The simplest of these is the existence of substantial transactions costs in buying and selling shares (especially in small lots), which makes the declaration of one's own dividends an expensive activity. Another reason is that, especially under certain tax systems, the tax liability of the company and its shareholders is affected by the level of the payout ratio.* For example, under the American corporation tax system, it would be costly for a shareholder to have to purchase additional shares out of 'excess' dividends, since this would

---

* This subject has received considerable attention elsewhere, and we shall accordingly devote little space to it here. See, for example, the discussion and references in King (1974a, b).

cause him to pay income taxes on these dividends. He would be better off were the company directly to retain such an excess. A third reason is that in practice firms do not pursue a neoclassical investment policy. In particular, since managers are motivated (for reasons discussed earlier) by a desire to increase the size of their firms, they may deliberately invest retained earnings in projects yielding less than the best return that shareholders could obtain were they to invest these funds outside the firm. In such cases, if the stock market were sufficiently well informed, the market value of the company's shares would rise by less than the amount of the retained earnings in question.

But of much greater importance than any of the reasons so far mentioned is the fact that shares are traded in an extraordinarily volatile and uncertain market. This is a fact which neoclassical economists consistently ignore, despite (or perhaps because of) making substantial use of formal models of share valuation. All such neoclassical models derive from the proposition that in equilibrium the price of a share is determined by the stream of expected future returns (dividends and capital gains), discounted at some appropriate rate. But in a world of great ignorance about the future, such a proposition (though undoubtedly correct) is remarkably unilluminating, for it fails to explain what determines expectations of future dividends and of future changes in share prices. And this is a question which cannot possibly be given a neat formal answer, especially in a speculative market in which the most significant expectations concern other people's expectations.

For in reality the stock market is dominated by the speculative activities of short term shareholders. There is, moreover, only a very limited amount of 'hard' information available, which causes an exaggerated importance to be attached to isolated scraps of information and unsubstantiated rumours. As a result, one observes wide and irregular fluctuations over time both in the average level of share prices and in the prices of individual shares relative to the average. These fluctuations are caused by the inextricably entangled effects of news of real events, speculative interdependence, and erratically changing expectations of a highly uncertain future. They are regarded as unpredictable by the great majority of shareholders. There is, indeed, a large school of thought which goes so far as to believe that the behaviour of share prices is best viewed as the outcome of a random process. At the very least, however, one may state without fear of contradiction that the price of a share in a company is a great deal more uncertain (ex ante) and volatile (ex post) than are the fortunes and profits of the company itself.

It is this above all else which vitiates the neoclassical view of dividend policy. To begin with, it means that shareholders cannot in practice freely declare their own dividends. For, since the stock market is volatile, shareholders will in all probability have to bear very substantial costs if they are obliged to buy or to sell shares at particular times, especially if they are obliged to buy when the market is high or to sell when the market is low. More generally, the volatility of the stock market means that the retention of earnings will not have a consistent and predictable effect on the market value of a company's shares, regardless of the way in which management is investing the retained earnings. This unpredictability is aggravated by the fact that both a company's shareholders and the stock market in general tend to be very badly informed about the future profitability of the investment being carried out within any particular company.

In consequence, other things (including the company's investment policy) being equal, the riskiness of a share is inversely related to the payout ratio of the company in question. That is, the greater the proportion of earnings which a company retains, the more uncertain will be the stream of returns from holding its shares. This, it should be stressed, is not because the company's investments (and the future profits from them) are uncertain. Nor, as some have suggested, is it simply because a low payout ratio increases the futurity of the company's dividend stream.* It is, rather, because the stock market's capitalisation of any particular stream of dividends and profits (of specified futurity and uncertainty) is itself inherently highly uncertain. As a result, dividends, by putting cash into the shareholder's hands, confer a benefit on him which is certain and tangible in a sense in which retained earnings, however lucratively invested, do not. For there

---

* Gordon (1962), especially ch. 5. Gordon, it should be noted, drew the right conclusion about dividend policy, but for the wrong reason. He was led astray, one suspects, by his desire to remain within the framework of formal neoclassical models of share valuation.

is no guarantee that the retention of earnings will enable the shareholder to realise a commensurate capital gain on his shares either in the period in which the profits are initially retained or in any specified subsequent period.

In practice, then, the character of the dividend decision is not at all that which is implied by the neoclassical model. In particular, shareholders do not regard dividend policy primarily in terms of the quality of the company's marginal investment opportunities. Instead, they view the payout decision pre-eminently as a decision about how much of the bird is to be put into the hand and how much is to be left in the bush. This is not to deny that shareholders may wish to have a substantial amount of the bird left in the bush. Nor can it be denied that their wishes in this regard may be to some extent affected by what they believe to be the scope for profitable internal investment, ill-informed though these beliefs may be. Other factors, however, are likely in reality to exert a much greater influence on shareholders' preferences about dividend policy. Four of these factors are of particular importance.

(1) The expectations of shareholders concerning the volatility and uncertainty of the stock market, as regards both the average level of share prices and the prices of individual shares relative to the average. For example, is a particular company a blue chip investment – in which case its relative share price is unlikely to be subject to major variations – or is it the type of concern about which opinions are liable to fluctuate? Clearly, the greater the expected volatility of the price of a company's shares, the greater will be the expected costs of being obliged to sell or to buy shares at particular times, and thus, other things being equal, the stronger will be the preference of shareholders for a high payout ratio.

(2) The degree of liquidity preference among shareholders (and in particular the strength of what Keynes called the transactions and precautionary motives). As it is used here, the term 'liquidity preference' is intended both to convey sentiments about the form in which wealth is held and to express needs for regular and guaranteed income as against irregular and uncertain receipts. These will depend on shareholders' expectations of the volume and pattern of their future expenditure requirements (including requirements whose extent and timing cannot accurately be foreseen),

45

and on the expected ease and cost of borrowing in the event of liquidity difficulties. In this connection, it must not be forgotten that the imperfection of capital markets affects shareholders as much as it does companies. Indeed, liquidity preference is a factor which acquires its force largely because shareholders, like companies, have to contend with finance (or cash flow) problems. Again, other things being equal, it is evident that the stronger a shareholder's liquidity preference, the more will he be inclined to favour a high payout ratio.

(3) The degree of risk aversion among shareholders. To what extent, in particular, are shareholders disposed to gamble by allowing the profits already earned by their companies to remain at the mercy of the stock exchange? This is partly a matter of temperament and partly a matter of the nature of the effects which gains or losses on the stock market may be expected to have on the shareholder's situation. Other things being equal, the less risk averse the shareholder, the lower will be his preferred payout ratio.

(4) The tax position of the shareholder and of the company (which has already been mentioned above). Of particular importance, for obvious reasons, is the impact of the payout ratio on the total amount of tax paid by the company and the shareholder.* This depends on a number of things, including the form of the company tax system, the tax rates, the income level of the shareholder, the rate at which the stock market is expected to capitalise retained earnings and the length of the interval which is expected to elapse between the accrual and the realisation of capital gains. It is clear that, other things being equal, the higher the effective relative tax rate on dividends, the stronger will be the shareholder's preference for a low payout ratio.

These are the fundamental considerations which managers must bear in mind if they wish to choose a payout ratio which is in the best interests of shareholders. There are, however, certain other factors which enter into the dividend decision. One of these is what are called the 'information effects' of dividend policy, being the effects which current dividends have on expectations of future dividends and earnings (see Lintner, 1956). These effects, which are of great importance in a world in which the supply of informa-

* See King (1974a, b) and the studies cited therein.

tion is very limited, are bound up with a powerful and self-perpetuating convention of dividend stabilisation.

Specifically, shareholders believe (correctly) that long run target payout ratios change by relatively little over considerable periods of time. They also believe (correctly) that companies endeavour to stabilise the level of dividends in the face of short run fluctuations of earnings (in effect by allowing the actual payout ratio to vary in the short run around its long run target). In consequence, shareholders interpret increases and decreases in current dividends as reflecting managerial expectations of long term increases and decreases in future earnings and dividends. As a result, for example, a company with exceptionally good investment opportunities which attempted to finance a burst of investment by cutting its current dividend would convince the stock market that its prospects were in fact bleak, and its share price would fall. It would appear, moreover, that the information effects of dividend changes are asymmetric; unexpected cuts in the dividend have a greater impact than unexpected increases.

Thus the information effects of dividends, which derive from this convention of dividend stabilisation, also contribute to its perpetuation. For managers are persuaded to maintain a stable level of dividends by the adverse effect which fluctuating dividends would have on the valuation ratio (and therefore on the interests of long run shareholders).* Cuts in the current dividend are avoided as far as possible, as are increases so large that they might have to be followed by subsequent cuts. It may be noted in passing that the information effects of dividend policy make it particularly costly for the shareholder to declare his own dividends. For a cut in the dividend (which would tend to make shareholders wish to sell shares) has an adverse effect on the share price, making it a bad time to sell, while a rise in the dividend (which would tend to make shareholders wish to buy shares) has a favourable effect on the share price, making it a bad time to buy.

One must also take account of the fact that managerial interests may exert an influence on the choice of a payout ratio. In par-

---

* Another reason for dividend stabilisation is that a record of fluctuating dividends would create expectations of fluctuations in the future which, by enhancing the uncertainty of the expected returns from a share, would exert a depressing effect on its price.

ticular, since managers are concerned mainly with increasing the size of their firms, they will be inclined to choose lower payout ratios than would be appropriate from the viewpoint of the welfare of long term shareholders. The extent to which they give expression to this inclination in practice is probably not very great; it depends on the efficacy of the mechanisms (discussed above) by which shareholder interests constrain managerial decisions with regard to dividend policy.

There is, however, another reason of a rather different kind why both managers and shareholders are likely to favour low payout ratios. This arises from the fact that dividend stabilisation amplifies the short run variability of retained profits in relation to the short run variability of profits, to an extent which depends on the level of the long run target payout ratio. The higher the target payout ratio, the greater is the proportional short run change in retained profits as a result of any given proportional short run change in profits. And the greater the variability of retained profits, the greater is the strain imposed on the firm's short run financial resources. Thus a high payout ratio would increase the risk that the firm's long run investment programme might be interrupted by a short run fall in profits, unless the firm were to hold a substantially greater proportion of its assets in liquid form. This consideration disposes companies to prefer lower payout ratios than would otherwise be appropriate. Its force depends on the expected variability of profits and on the expected availability of short term credit facilities. For instance, firms (such as those in the capital goods industries) whose profits are subject to greater than average fluctuations tend to choose lower than average payout ratios.*

It is clear, then, that managers must take account of a number of different factors in choosing a target payout ratio. Of particular importance are the preferences and interests of the long term shareholder, especially his expectations of the volatility of the stock market, his degree of liquidity preference, his degree of risk aversion, his tax position and his views of the quality of the

* Cf. Gordon (1962) p. 231, and Singh and Whittington (1968) pp. 39–41. Moreover, since such firms also tend to choose lower than average gearing ratios (for the reasons discussed on p. 32 above), this accounts for the fact that a positive correlation is observed in cross-section between the payout ratio and the gearing ratio.

company's investment opportunities. But shareholders are far from homogeneous in these various respects. As a result, different shareholders prefer different payout ratios, a fact which gives rise to two serious problems for managers. One of these is how to obtain information about the preferences of shareholders, especially since there is no practicable means of direct enquiry and since the price of a company's shares is at any moment an unreliable guide to the views of its long term shareholders. The other problem is how to reconcile the conflicting interests of different groups of shareholders. At the same time, in choosing a target payout ratio, managers must weigh their own interests against the interests of shareholders, pay due regard to the information content of dividends, and keep in mind the variability of the company's profits and the extent of its short run financial resources.

Dividend policy is therefore a matter of considerable complexity, and managers are inevitably faced with certain difficulties in deciding on an appropriate payout ratio. In practice, the principal response to these difficulties consists of the maintenance of relatively constant target payout ratios over very long periods of time.* There are a number of reasons for this. One is simply that a standard response to complicated decisions is to employ a rule of thumb, and that a particular rule of thumb, once chosen, tends to perpetuate itself through sheer inertia (cf. Cyert and March, 1963). But there are other, more powerful, reasons for stable target payout ratios.

The most important of these are what we may call 'clientele effects'. For it is essential to recognise that the nature of a company's shareholders is not independent of the policies pursued by its management. Indeed, it would probably be more accurate to say that the nature of a company's shareholders adapts itself to the policies of management than to say that the policies pursued by management adapt themselves to the nature of the company's shareholders. Specifically, shareholders who, for the sorts of reasons discussed earlier, prefer a high payout ratio will buy shares in companies with high payout ratios, while shareholders who prefer a low payout ratio will buy the shares of companies

---

* A phenomenon which, together with short run dividend stabilisation (or 'partial adaptation'), has been abundantly documented. See, for example, Lintner (1956), Kuh (1963), Brittain (1964, 1966), and Turnovsky (1967).

with low payout ratios.* This reduces the diversity of preferences among the shareholders of any given company, which goes some way towards resolving certain of the problems described above. However, such behaviour on the part of shareholders is possible only if companies pursue consistent payout policies over long periods of time. In particular, if a company were unexpectedly to change its payout ratio, it would inflict costs upon its clientele of shareholders by obliging them to make unanticipated sales and purchases of shares. In any given company, then, the target payout ratio which has prevailed in the past is in effect the basis of a contract between managers and long term shareholders which cannot lightly be breached.

Much the same may be said in connection with conflicts of interest between managers and shareholders with regard to the level of the payout ratio. For the shareholders of a particular company cannot reasonably complain if management continues to pursue a payout policy which was anticipated by shareholders when they bought their shares. Dissatisfaction among shareholders would arise, however, if management were to break the implied contract by, for example, making an otherwise unjustified cut in the level of the payout ratio. In practice, then, once it is established, the payout ratio becomes a variable of secondary importance in the eyes of shareholders. Far more attention is paid to the other determinant of the level of dividends, namely the absolute level of the company's earnings. In consequence, the conflict of interest between managers and shareholders over the level of the payout ratio tends to remain latent.

There are, therefore, forces which cause target payout ratios to remain relatively constant over long periods of time, and there is accordingly a sense in which a company's target payout ratio is at any moment of time arbitrarily determined.† But it would be an

* The same considerations which dictate a preference for a high payout ratio will of course lead some investors to eschew shares altogether and to invest in bonds. Moreover, shareholders will be influenced in their choice of shares not only by the payout ratios of the companies concerned, but also by their beliefs about the company's profit and growth prospects and about the volatility of the company's share price. These beliefs, since they tend to be held in common by the shareholders of a company, constitute another reason for describing a company's shareholders as a particular clientele.

† It is therefore unsurprising that the pattern of payout ratios exhibited by

exaggeration to suggest that payout ratios are necessarily strictly constant over time, and it would thus be inaccurate to maintain that in the long run they are wholly arbitrarily determined. For gradual alterations in the levels of the payout ratios chosen by managers are caused by changes in the various factors which were described above as exerting an influence on dividend policy. Examples of such alterations spring readily to mind (although the following list is not intended to be exhaustive).

(1) Changes in systems and rates of taxation. For example, changes in the company tax system which increase the degree of discrimination against dividends have been observed to have a depressing effect on payout ratios, as have increases in rates of personal income tax in upper income brackets.* (2) Managerial expectations of a secular reduction in the amplitude of short run cycles of activity in the economy would tend to raise payout ratios. (3) Measures designed to reduce the volatility of the stock market, such as an increase in the stamp duty on transactions, might tend to reduce payout ratios. (4) It is also possible that a firm's payout ratio might be affected by a radical change in the character of the investment opportunities confronting it. For example, a firm which foresaw a long term improvement in its prospects (not necessarily in relation to any external yardstick, but in relation

a cross-section of companies at any moment of time is rather incoherent. There are, for example, few systematic relationships between the level of the payout ratio and other measurable characteristics of companies (an exception to this being the relationship already mentioned between the payout ratio, the variability of profits and the gearing ratio). The payout ratios of individual companies appear to be independent of their (average) profit rates, and this (together with the limited importance of external finance) renders it plausible that the payout ratios of individual companies should be weakly negatively correlated with their growth rates. Cf. Gordon (1962), and Singh and Whittington (1968).

* On the former subject, see King (1974a), and the references therein. On the latter, see Brittain (1966). Brittain also discovered that payout ratios (measured using data on profits net of depreciation allowances for tax purposes) were affected by the liberality of depreciation allowances for tax purposes. The explanation of this result, however, is almost certainly that companies, in making payout ratio decisions, measure their profits net of depreciation as calculated on some other basis. Specifically, it is likely that the depreciation rules employed by company accountants vary less over time than do the depreciation rules employed by the tax authorities; cf. Brittain (1966), p. 200.

to its own past investment opportunities) might move towards a lower payout ratio. (5) In a rather different vein, one should mention that payout ratios are also liable to change in response to various sorts of government-imposed restrictions on dividend payments.

The general drift of the present discussion of dividend policy is intended to apply both to quoted and to unquoted companies. However, since the exposition has revolved around quoted companies, it is perhaps worth adding a few words about the special peculiarities of unquoted companies. Clearly, the volatility of the stock market as such can have no influence on the dividend policy of an unquoted company. However, it is necessarily exceedingly costly, if not downright impossible, for the shareholders of an unquoted company to declare their own dividends. The liquidity preference of shareholders is therefore likely to have if anything a greater influence on the dividend policy of unquoted companies. Indeed, the choice of a payout ratio in an unquoted company may become closely bound up with personal propensities to consume and save (as of course is the case with entrepreneurial withdrawals from unincorporated firms). At the same time, the shareholders of unquoted companies will tend to have greater control over the dividend decision, and they may tend also to be better informed about a company's investment opportunities. Thus dividend policy in unquoted companies, while fundamentally similar to dividend policy in quoted companies, is inevitably subject to certain differences of emphasis.

2.5 NEW ISSUES OF ORDINARY SHARES

There remains undiscussed one further source of company finance, namely new issues of ordinary shares. In this regard, we shall consider only what are called 'new money' issues, being those which increase the amount of finance available to companies. Thus we shall disregard 'capitalisation' or 'scrip' issues. Moreover, for the reasons given earlier, we shall ignore new issues made in exchange for the shares of other companies in the course of mergers and takeovers.*

* To which, it should be noted, the three considerations discussed on pp. 55–6 below are virtually irrelevant (although they do apply to new issues made in

In addition, although we shall turn to the subject of unquoted companies towards the end of the section, most of the discussion will concern new issues by companies whose shares are already quoted on the stock market. Such issues, which constitute the bulk of new money issues, normally take the form of 'rights' issues, whereby the existing shareholders of a company are given a pre-emptive right to subscribe to its new shares.* In the present context, however, the technicalities of the method of issue are not of great importance.†

It is notable that in practice new issues of shares are a very minor source of finance.‡ That is, companies rarely make new issues, and when they do, the sums raised are comparatively small. To some extent this is because companies are deterred by the inconvenience and the administrative and brokerage costs involved in making an issue.§ But the principal reason for the rarity of new issues is that they are disliked by long term shareholders. For, to put the matter in its simplest form, a new issue, by increasing the supply of a company's shares, tends to drive down the share price and inflict a capital loss on the company's existing shareholders.‖

connection with the other sorts of mergers and acquisitions discussed on pp. 20–3 above). Specifically, it is much easier to persuade investors to submit, in effect, to a change in the name of a company than to persuade them actually to purchase additional shares for cash.

* This is invariably the case in the U.K., both because stock exchange regulations oblige a company to use this method unless its shareholders have voted to the contrary and because the administrative and underwriting costs of rights issues are much lower than those of issues made by other methods.

† A good exposition of the various alternative methods of making new issues is to be found in Merrett, Howe and Newbould (1967).

‡ For example, for a large sample of U.K. quoted companies over the period 1967–70 inclusive, new money issues of ordinary shares constituted only 2.4 per cent of total uses of funds (net of expenditure on the acquisition of subsidiaries); *Annual Abstract of Statistics* 1972, Table 396. The situation in the U.S. is similar; see Gordon (1962) pp. 124 and 230. In continental Europe there is even less reliance on new issues of shares; see Economic Research Group of Amsterdam–Rotterdam Bank (1966).

§ The issuing costs of a rights issue in the U.K. average 2.5 per cent of the proceeds of the issue; Merrett, Howe and Newbould (1967) ch. 3. The issuing costs of rights issues are substantially higher in the U.S.; Merrett and Sykes (1964) p. 92.

‖ With regard to a rights issue, it should be stressed that the capital loss in question is caused by a fall in the *cum-rights* price. More particularly, the fall

This consideration, though in one sense straightforward and obvious, deserves closer attention, not least because it would be of no relevance in the simplest sort of neoclassical model of equilibrium in a perfect stock market in a world of certainty with no taxes or transactions costs (see, for example, Modigliani and Miller, 1967, p. 190). For in such a model, whether long term shareholders liked or disliked a new issue would depend solely on whether the rate of return on the investment to be financed by the new issue was greater or less than the prevailing interest rate (this being the rate at which future returns from owning the company's shares would be discounted by the market).* In the former case, a new issue would confer a capital gain on existing shareholders, since the stock market value of the company would increase by more than the proceeds of the new issue; in the latter case, a new issue would inflict a capital loss.† Thus shareholders would have no reason to dislike new issues in general; their attitude would depend exclusively on the nature of the use to which the proceeds of any particular new issue were to be put.

Needless to say, there are many respects in which this simple neoclassical model is not an accurate description of reality. The one which is of fundamental importance in the present context is that the stock market is not perfect, in the specific sense that the price of a share in any period is not independent of the number of shares offered for sale in that period. In particular, all other things being equal (including the company's objective situation and behaviour, the market's opinions of its prospects and the size of the total stock of its shares in issue), an increase in the number

in the cum-rights price caused by a new issue should not be confused with the fact that (for reasons connected with the technicalities of the method of issue) the ex-rights price is normally lower than the cum-rights price. For a fuller discussion of this point see n* on p. 55 below.

* Since the prevailing interest rate would be the rate of return that investors would earn on any alternative investment.

† The total capital gain or loss to existing shareholders being simply the net present value of the investment in question discounted at the ruling interest rate. For the stock market value of the company will rise by the *gross* present value of the investment, from which one must subtract the value of the new issue (which is identically equal to the investment outlay involved) to arrive at the gain or loss to existing shareholders.

of shares offered for sale will depress the share price. To put the matter another way, it is the case in practice that in order to sell a new issue an incentive is required to persuade investors to introduce the new shares into their portfolios. The necessary incentive is provided by an increase in the expected rate of return on the company's shares above what it would otherwise have been, which is achieved by a reduction in the share price below what it would otherwise have been.*

It is worth explaining in more detail why the demand for the shares of a particular company is imperfectly elastic with respect to price; why, that is, it is necessary for a company's shares to become more attractive in order to sell a new issue. There are a number of reasons, all of which stem in one way or another from the ignorance of investors about the future.

(1) Because the extent and timing of new issues cannot be foreseen with any accuracy (the more so because new issues are so rare), a *rearrangement* of portfolios and portfolio plans is required if the market is to absorb the increased supply of shares. To pay for the new shares, investors must sell or refrain from buying an equivalent amount of other shares (or other investments or consumption goods). The impediments to such a rearrangement are

* This, it should be noted, has nothing to do with the 'discount' at which rights issues are offered to existing shareholders. In a rights issue, the nominal price at which new shares are sold is virtually irrelevant: it should have no effect either on the level of the future rate of return expected on the company's shares or on the extent of the capital loss inflicted on existing shareholders by the issue. (For a fuller discussion, see Merrett, Howe and Newbould (1967) pp. 49–51). Nor indeed does the discount make the new shares any cheaper to existing shareholders than to new shareholders, since both effectively pay the ex-rights price for the new shares. (An existing shareholder pays the nominal price plus the value of the foregone opportunity to sell his right; a new shareholder pays the nominal price plus the price of the right he has had to buy from an existing shareholder). There has been some suggestion, though, that shareholders are misinformed in this regard. In particular, on the basis of an empirical study, Edge (1965) concluded that the extent of the discount influences existing shareholders' decisions on whether to exercise or to sell their rights. It is possible, however, that the causation in question is the reverse of that supposed by Edge; that is, that the effective size of the discount is partly determined by the extent to which shareholders sell their rights rather than exercising them (since this might affect the degree to which the share price falls as a result of a rights issue).

(a) the transactions costs involved, (b) the inconvenience of altering portfolio or expenditure plans and (c) what might be called 'portfolio inertia' (especially among long term shareholders, who tend to stick to particular portfolios over considerable periods of time and are very insensitive to short term movements of share prices). Some incentive is clearly necessary to overcome these impediments.

(2) Moreover, as was explained in an earlier section, different investors normally entertain a range of different expectations about the stream of returns from any given share. Thus at any particular price, different investors will regard a given share as offering different rates of return. A company's clientele of shareholders is accordingly composed of those investors who hold the most favourable views of the stream of returns to be expected from its shares (in relation to their expectations of other shares). Other investors, whose expectations, relatively speaking, are less favourable, will prefer to hold the shares of other companies. However, given the expectations of investors about the stream of returns from the share in question, a reduction in its price will increase the rates of return expected by all investors. This in turn will cause some hitherto extra-marginal shareholders to substitute this share for other shares in their portfolios. In effect, then, one way of selling a new issue is by luring relatively pessimistic shareholders into a company's clientele.

(3) There is of course another way in which a new issue can be sold, which is by persuading a company's existing shareholders to increase their holdings above what they would otherwise have been. However, the greater the extent to which a portfolio is concentrated on the shares of a few companies, the greater the attendant degree of risk. In consequence, an increase in the rate of return expected on a company's shares is necessary to induce its existing shareholders to submit to the extra risks of expanding their holdings.

These, then, are the reasons why the attractiveness of a company's shares must improve if a new issue is to be taken up by the stock market. By the same token, since the necessary incentive must be provided by a reduction in the price of the company's shares below what it would otherwise have been, they are the reasons why, other things being equal, a new issue inflicts a capital loss on existing shareholders.* However, other things are not necessarily equal. In particular, if the new issue in and of itself were to cause an improvement of expectations about the stream of returns (per share) from the shares of the company in question, this would tend to push up the share price, possibly to an extent great enough to offset completely the sort of depressing tendency described above. If this were the case, because for example the market believed that the proceeds of the issue were to be applied to some particularly lucrative project, shareholders might derive a capital gain from the new issue despite the need to provide an incentive for the market to take it up.†

In order for a new issue to confer a net gain on shareholders, it is essential not only that managers should regard the project concerned as exceptionally profitable, but that investors should agree with them, and that investors should believe that other investors will be similarly impressed. This requires, of course, that investors be accurately informed about the profitability of a company's investment opportunities, which in practice they are not. Indeed, it is normally very difficult for managers to convince the stock market of an impending revolution in a company's fortunes. Furthermore, the 'information effects' of a new issue need not be favourable, and if a new issue *per se* caused expectations to deteriorate, the losses of existing shareholders would be compounded. Such a deterioration of expectations might occur because one new issue created an expectation that there would be further new issues, or because the stock market believed that the inability of the company to finance its investment by retaining profits and borrowing presaged low future profits.

In general, it would appear that the 'information effect' of new

---

* Moreover, it is clear from what has been said that the larger is the new issue, the larger will be the fall in the share price below what it would otherwise have been, and thus, other things being equal, the greater will be the loss inflicted on existing shareholders.

† It must be stressed that an improvement in expectations of this kind cannot in itself provide the incentive necessary to sell the new issue. For it will simply raise the price of the company's shares to a level such that a purchaser would earn a 'normal' rate of return. In order to attract purchasers, by contrast, the rate of return must be above normal; that is, the share price must be below what it would have been had a similar improvement in expectations occurred in the absence of a new issue.

issues is not sufficient to offset the adverse effects of an increase in supply. For, in practice, the mere announcement of an impending new issue will depress the price of a company's shares (Merrett, Howe and Newbould, 1967, pp. 58–9). In general, therefore, companies simply do not make new issues, since managers (as was argued earlier) are particularly sensitive to the welfare of shareholders in this regard. In exceptional circumstances, however, a company will make a new issue, although even then it will be anxious to limit the size of the issue. The circumstances in question arise when a company has a strong reason for undertaking a substantial burst of investment which is out of line with the established trend of its investment expenditures. This occurs most commonly as a result of a breakthrough in sales prospects which would permit a rapid but temporary phase of expansion. Companies are sometimes also faced with a pressing need to implement a sudden programme of modernisation and replacement in order to prevent a deterioration in their competitive positions.

It is normally in the interests of both managers and long term shareholders that such opportunities should be seized, in the sense that this sort of burst of investment would have a favourable effect both on the size of the firm and on the level of its future earnings. And if such a burst of investment were to be undertaken, a new issue might be an appropriate way to obtain the necessary finance. For, given the company's gearing limit, only a proportion of the investment could be financed by increased borrowing, and to increase retained earnings by enough to finance the remainder would be undesirable for reasons discussed in the previous section because it would require a marked reduction in the payout ratio (and quite possibly a cut in the absolute level of the current dividend).

Thus although a company may make some reduction in its payout ratio in these circumstances, beyond a certain point it will do less damage to the interests of its shareholders by making a new issue. There are two reasons for this. First, although a new issue tends to inflict a capital loss on shareholders, a capital loss would also be caused by the adverse information effects of a reduction in the rate of growth of dividends, especially if the absolute level of the dividend were cut. Secondly, a new issue has a less damaging effect on the liquidity position of shareholders than a reduction in dividends. For, even though a shareholder may in fact decide to subscribe to a rights issue, it does at least give him the choice of whether or not to contribute to the financing of the burst of investment. Furthermore, if a new issue were made as a result of exceptional opportunities of the type described, there would be a better chance that the depressing effect of the issue on the company's share price would be wholly or partly offset by an improvement in the stock market's expectations of the company's prospects.*

It should also be noted that a high valuation ratio makes a new issue of shares less disadvantageous to shareholders. For the higher is a company's valuation ratio, the smaller is the proportional increase in the number of its shares in issue which would be needed in order to finance any given proportional expansion of its assets, and thus, other things being equal, the less will its share price be depressed.† To some extent this may influence the behaviour of individual companies in cross-section. But its main effect is on the timing of new issues; more new issues are made in stock market booms, when valuation ratios tend to be high, and fewer are made in stock market slumps, when valuation ratios are lower. (In consequence, companies intending to make a new issue frequently build up short term debt while awaiting a suitable moment to float the issue and devote the immediate proceeds of the issue to repaying this debt – cf. Tew and Henderson, 1959, p. 83).

Finally, something must be said about unquoted companies. Such companies can of course 'go public' and raise finance by

---

* There is little systematic empirical information on the behaviour of companies with regard to new issues, presumably because new issues are so rare. It is clear that (in cross-section) reliance on external finance in general and new issues in particular is associated with exceptional growth (see Tew and Henderson, 1959, ch. 5; Singh and Whittington, 1968, ch. 3 and pp. 177–83; Kuh, 1963, ch. 11; Meyer and Kuh, 1959, ch. IX; and Gordon, 1962, p. 230). However, not all studies have disentangled the contribution to this relationship which is made by growth by merger. Of considerable additional interest, though, is Whittington's (1971, pp. 136–40) finding that the use of external funds tends to be associated with a subsequent increase in a company's profitability.

† Kaldor (1970a) p. 250. Consider, for example, a company which wishes to finance a 10 per cent expansion of its assets by a new issue. If its valuation ratio (ex post) were 4, the required proportional increase in the number of its shares in issue would be 2.5 per cent, while if its valuation ratio were 2, the required proportional increase in the number of its shares would be 5 per cent.

3-2

a new issues of shares.* But the deterrents to new issues of this kind are if anything more serious than those which affect quoted companies. To begin with, the administrative and brokerage costs of a new issue by a new company are proportionately much greater than those of a rights issue by a previously quoted company (Merrett, Howe and Newbould, 1967, p. 181). Even more important is the fact that many unquoted companies are family firms which are extremely reluctant to expand the ownership of the firm outside the family.† As a result, yet more exceptional opportunities are needed to induce an unquoted company to make a new issue. There are, in addition, various sources other than the public issue of shares from which an unquoted company might obtain new equity capital, including merchant banks, certain government-sponsored agencies and individual directors and members of the family. But in aggregate these sources of funds make a negligibly small contribution to the finances of the company sector.

* Such new issues should not be confused with the process of making the company's existing shares available to a wider public.

† As reported, for example, in many of the case studies in Mackintosh (1963).

3

THE LONG RUN PROFIT MARGIN

In this chapter we shall explain what determines the long run profit margin of the individual firm. By 'long run' we mean not only 'strategic' in the general sense discussed earlier, but also, more specifically, 'at normal full capacity use'. For, since capacity is in the long run a variable within the firm's control, it will formulate its strategic plans with a view to maintaining some normal relationship between demand and capacity. In the short run, however, when capacity is in effect fixed, the firm will expect the degree of capacity use to fluctuate in a comparatively unpredictable way with fluctuations in demand. Such fluctuations, for reasons to be discussed later in the chapter, will tend to cause the firm's actual profit margin to vary in the short run around its target long run profit margin. But our principal concern is with the long run profit margin itself.

We are taking it for granted that firms do in fact have long run perspectives of their future development and that the profit margin decision is essentially a long run decision which is not directly affected by short run vagaries of demand. This view is supported by a great deal of evidence both on the behaviour of companies in general and on the nature of their profit margin decisions. In particular, most empirical studies have shown that industrial and commercial companies set their prices on the basis of a proportional mark-up on unit costs, the latter being calculated at normal full capacity use, and that the size of the mark-up is invariant with respect to short run changes in the degree of capacity use.* In effect, then, the object of the present chapter is to explain what determines the size of this target mark-up.

* The most celebrated such study is Hall and Hitch (1939). See also Godley and Nordhaus (1972), and Cyert and March (1963), and the references cited in these works. It should perhaps be noted that, unlike Hall and Hitch, we are regarding non-capital overhead costs as an element of unit costs rather than as an element of the mark-up.

For convenience, however, we shall define the profit margin not as the mark-up on costs but as its close relation, the ratio of profits to sales revenue.* It should perhaps be pointed out that the profit margin of the individual company, which is our main concern, is not the same thing as the profit margin on an individual product, except in the rather unusual case of a one-product firm. But in the present context it is appropriate to focus on 'high level' variables such as the average profit margin on a company's products, its total sales revenue and its total investment expenditure, and to neglect the details of the production and sale of individual commodities. It would not be difficult to embody the principles of the present theory in a model which dealt also with individual price, output, input, selling cost and investment decisions (which depend mainly on a number of very orthodox considerations connected with the firm's desire to be efficient in various familiar senses).† But such a model would be unnecessarily complicated for the purpose at hand. For our principal interest lies in explaining the distribution of income rather than, say, the relative price and output levels of individual commodities.

A fundamental assumption of the present theory is that the basic goal of those in charge of the firm is to cause its sales revenue to grow as rapidly as possible, subject to certain constraints. The constraints in question are the growth of demand, the growth of capacity and the availability of finance for investment. These three types of constraint are central to the present theory. We shall begin by discussing them separately. Thus in the next section of this chapter, under the heading of 'the opportunity frontier', we shall explore the relationships between the profit margin of the firm and the demand for its products, and between its investment expenditures and its capacity to supply that demand.

* Let the mark-up be MU and the ratio of profits to sales revenue be π: by definition, $MU = \pi/(1-\pi)$. Incidentally, it makes no difference of principle in the context of the present theory whether companies set their prices on a 'historical cost' basis (which corresponds to the valuation of stocks on the 'first in, first out' principle) or on a 'replacement cost' basis (which corresponds to the valuation of stocks on the 'last in, first out' principle), although the details of the outcome predicted by the theory will, of course, depend on which convention is adopted; see p. 11 above and Godley and Nordhaus (1972).

† In this connection, see Baumol (1967) ch. 7 and Mathematical Notes, and Lintner (1971) pp. 182–5.

In the following section we shall summarise the conclusions reached in chapter 2 concerning the relationship between the profits of the firm and the availability of finance for its investment expenditures.

We shall then assemble a complete model of the individual firm, proceeding from a simple but abstract version of the model towards a more complex but more realistic framework. To begin with, we shall assume that the profit margin decision is taken within a single long planning period. Later on, we shall adopt the more relevant context of a series of long planning periods which are not discrete but which overlap with and shade into one another. We shall call this a 'dynamic' context, by contrast with the 'static' single-period context. Moreover, although we shall start with the assumption of equilibrium in the sense that the firm's expectations of the future are more or less fulfilled, we shall enquire towards the end of the chapter into the way in which firms behave in the face of disequilibrium. This enquiry will provide a convenient basis for a further discussion of the relationship between behaviour in the long run and behaviour in the short run.

3.2 THE OPPORTUNITY FRONTIER

In this section we shall pay no attention to the availability of finance. We shall investigate instead the firm's *opportunities* to invest, to sell its products and to make profits, postponing until the next section all discussion of financial constraints on investment.

Consider the situation of the managers of a single company looking ahead over a single long planning period. The opportunities which they perceive as being open to the company may be described as a set of possible alternative strategies, which we shall call the 'opportunity set'. A strategy is defined as a particular bundle of price and output levels, sales policies, investment projects and so forth, which is feasible in the sense that the investment involved would provide capacity appropriate to the growth of demand that would occur if the strategy were to be implemented.

Given the nature of available technology and the expected prices of the various sorts of inputs (including labour and capital goods), each strategy is associated with (a) a particular average profit margin on the firm's sales, (b) a particular growth rate of its total sales revenue (in relation to sales in the preceding period) and (c) a particular level of total investment expenditure. (Thus the simplest way to characterise the opportunity set is as a region in three-dimensional space, each specific strategy being represented by a specific three-component vector.)

The opportunity set is bounded. That is, there are upper limits on the profit margin which the firm can attain, upper limits on the amount it can sell, and lower limits on the amount of investment it must undertake. These three sorts of limit, which are in various ways interdependent, constitute the frontier of the opportunity set, which we shall call the 'opportunity frontier'. The characteristics of the opportunity frontier (which may be thought of as a three-dimensional surface) are of special importance because, for reasons that will become more apparent later, the firm will always choose a strategy which lies on the frontier.* That is to say, other things being equal, managers will always prefer a strategy with a higher profit margin to one with a lower profit margin, a strategy with a higher growth rate of sales to one with a lower growth rate of sales, and a strategy involving a smaller investment outlay to one involving a larger investment outlay.

Discussion of the opportunity frontier is rendered complicated by the fact that we are dealing with a relationship between three variables. We shall accordingly proceed in stages, discussing first the relationship between the growth of demand for a company's products and its profit margin and second the relationship between investment outlays, increases in productive capacity and efficiency (in a sense to be defined below). We shall then combine these relationships and make some further comments on the nature of the opportunity frontier, with particular reference to the impact of uncertainty.

(i) *Demand growth*

In considering the individual firm we shall assume that the growth of aggregate demand in the economy is exogenously given.† The

---

* The conditions for being on the opportunity frontier (in terms of the price and output levels of individual commodities, selling cost levels, input mix and detailed investment expenditure levels) are mainly of a straightforward and familiar kind; see n † on p. 62 above.

† It is of course true that the individual company's investment and production affect aggregate demand and thus the demand for its own products. How-

growth of demand for the products of the individual firm therefore depends primarily on the effectiveness of its selling policies, especially in relation to the selling policies of the other firms with which it competes. Specifically, the growth of demand for a firm's products over any long period is determined by its choice of product mix (including its product innovations), by the quality of its products, by the price levels it sets and by the extent of its advertising and promotion expenditures of all kinds. The relative effectiveness of alternative selling policies depends on the rates of growth of the various available markets, on the nature of the products involved and on the policies pursued by rival companies.*

The firm's selling policy not only determines the rate of growth of demand for its products; it also exerts a major influence on the size of its profit margin (and it should be reiterated that we refer throughout to the long run or full capacity profit margin). One obvious way in which this occurs is through the choice of price levels; other things being equal, the lower are the firm's prices, the lower will be its profit margin. Similarly, the firm's selling policy will largely determine its unit costs; its choice of product mix and of quality levels will affect its production costs, the scale of its advertising and promotion efforts will affect its selling costs, and the extent to which it introduces new products will affect the level of its development expenditures. Other things being equal, of course, the higher the firm's unit costs, the lower will be its profit margin.

Among alternative selling policies, some will clearly be superior

ever, in the type of economy with which we are concerned, the impact of even the largest company's investment and production on the demand for its own products is so small that we can reasonably neglect it. To neglect it altogether is merely an assumption of convenience, and to incorporate it explicitly would not alter the substance of the present analysis.

* It will be noted that we avoid an explicit discussion of oligopolistic interdependence and the problems which this poses in the context of models of maximising behaviour. This should not be construed as a suggestion that businessmen overlook the reactions of their rivals in evaluating the outcomes of alternative selling policies. Nor should it be taken as a denial of the potential complexity of oligopolistic inter-reactions. It reflects instead a belief that in practice businessmen regard oligopolistic interdependence not as a peculiarly intractable problem but rather as one among many aspects of uncertainty about the future outcomes of alternative strategies. The more general issue of uncertainty is discussed towards the end of this section.

to others in that they would enable the firm to attain both a greater growth of demand and a higher profit margin. But beyond a certain point, the larger the amount by which the company tries to increase the demand for its products over the period, the smaller will be its best attainable profit margin. That is, the firm will encounter one aspect of the opportunity frontier, along which there is a tradeoff between high sales growth and a high profit margin.* The tradeoff exists because the firm is competing in various ways with other firms for a limited total amount of demand. The extra advertising, promotion, product innovation and quality improvement necessary to increase the demand for the company's products cause its unit costs to rise, and its prices cannot limitlessly be raised in proportion without adversely affecting demand.

The location of the demand–profit margin tradeoff (i.e. the size of the best attainable profit margin which is associated with any particular growth rate of demand) depends in large part on the company's 'efficiency' relative to other companies (as well as on a number of other factors to be discussed below). Efficiency in this sense comprises (a) selling efficiency, being the choice of effective selling policies, including the choice of product mix, and (b) cost efficiency, in the more usual sense of minimising the expenses incurred in implementing any particular selling policy.† Thus a company may have a relatively unfavourable demand–profit margin tradeoff either because it makes poor product mix, pricing and promotion decisions, or because it has high unit costs in production and in its marketing and other divisions. The standard of a company's performance in these various respects will in turn depend very heavily on the quality of its management.

* It may be noted in passing that a tradeoff of this kind would not necessarily exist if price competition were the only available form of competition; for (assuming constant unit operating costs for simplicity) if the demand curve were sufficiently inelastic, reductions in the profit margin would decrease sales revenue rather than increasing it. But in the real world, where non-price competition is of great importance, there will always be a tradeoff between high sales growth and a high profit margin, in effect because the firm can always shift its demand curve by varying the level of its selling expenditures.

† Note, however, that companies are cost minimisers only relative to a given selling policy – they may deliberately incur high selling costs and hence choose absolutely high unit costs.

66

(ii) *Investment, capacity growth and efficiency*

Increased demand enables the firm to expand its sales only if it has adequate capacity. The expansion of capacity requires investment in fixed capital and in stocks. Thus the level of investment expenditure which is needed for purposes of capacity expansion in any particular long period is determined by (a) the extent of the increase in output required to satisfy the increase in the demand for the company's products, (b) the company's views as to what is the appropriate or normal long run relationship between demand and capacity,* (c) the extent of excess capacity at the beginning of the period and (d) the amount of investment expenditure required to provide a unit increase in capacity in each individual product line.†

But investment is more than a passive variable whose level is determined by the need to provide capacity for an independently given increase in demand. For the level of investment expenditure is also a determinant of the extent of the increase in demand, since it influences the efficiency of the firm in both the senses described above. Not least, additional expenditure on the modification and replacement of production and sales facilities enables greater changes to be made in the product mix, which increases the degree to which the firm can improve its demand–profit margin tradeoff by replacing its existing products with other products for which demand is growing more rapidly or which can be sold at a higher profit margin. Moreover, the use of more capital intensive techniques in individual product lines (i.e. increasing the amount

* Which will depend on its expectations of cyclical, seasonal or erratic fluctuations in demand, on the costs of stockholding, and on its attitudes towards such things as overtime and short-time working, shiftwork and sub-contracting.

† One should perhaps add 'physical collapse of existing plant' to the list. But in general we shall assume that the economic life of equipment is shorter than its physical life, especially since the physical life of equipment can be protracted almost indefinitely by unlimited expenditure on maintenance (which we are treating as an operating cost). Strictly speaking, one should also add 'changes in the cost of stocks and work in progress' to the list. For since company accountants in Britain value stocks on a 'first in, first out' basis, a rising general price level makes some 'investment' in stocks necessary in each period merely to maintain a constant volume of stocks; see p. 1n above.

of investment expenditure per unit increase in capacity) will usually enable unit operating costs to be reduced, as will additional expenditure on the replacement of older equipment used to produce established products. A higher level of investment expenditure (both in providing new capacity and in replacing old capacity) might enable improvements to be made in product quality. And increased investment in stocks of inputs and outputs reduces the risks of lost sales due to interruptions in production or unexpected surges of demand.

Investment expenditure thus plays a double role, a fact of which companies are well aware.* On the one hand it provides the extra capacity needed to supply any given increase in demand. On the other, it is a way of improving the firm's efficiency or 'trade position' – a weapon in the competitive struggle to attract demand at the expense of other firms. Indeed, it is this latter aspect of investment expenditure which causes the opportunity frontier to possess a third dimension, in addition to the tradeoff identified above between demand growth and the profit margin.

For the location of the demand–profit margin tradeoff necessarily depends to a significant extent on the amount of investment carried out by the firm. That is, given any particular growth rate of demand, the size of the best attainable profit margin can be increased by additional investment expenditure or decreased by reduced investment expenditure. Correspondingly, given any particular level of the profit margin, the best attainable growth rate of demand can be increased or decreased by augmenting or diminishing the amount of investment. There are, of course, a whole range of strategies within the opportunity frontier, in choosing among which there need be no conflict between considerations of investment expense and considerations of efficiency. In other words, some strategies are superior to others in every respect. But once the frontier is attained, increased investment is necessary to improve the profit margin without adversely affecting the growth of demand or to improve the growth of demand without adversely affecting the profit margin. In effect, then, there also exists a second sort of tradeoff, between improving the

---

* See, for example, the survey of empirical literature on investment policy in Meyer and Kuh (1959), and the discussions of investment behaviour in Williams and Scott (1965), and in Barna (1962).

demand–profit margin tradeoff and keeping down the level of investment expenditure.

(iii) *The opportunity frontier formalised*

Let us now combine the two sorts of tradeoff into a single formal expression which represents the opportunity frontier of the individual firm in a particular long planning period. This could be done in various ways. The most convenient, in the present context, is by means of a function of the form

$$\pi \leqslant \mu(g, k)$$

where

π = the profit margin (profits, P, as a ratio of sales revenue, V).

g = the proportional growth in sales revenue $((V - \tilde{V})/V$, where $\tilde{V}$ is the level of sales revenue in the preceding period, which is exogenously determined by historical considerations).* This proportional measure of growth is in various respects more suitable for our purposes than an absolute measure of growth.

k = the 'investment coefficient' (investment expenditure, I, as a ratio of the absolute increase in sales revenue, $(V - \tilde{V})$). This variable (which is simply the gross incremental capital-output ratio) expresses the level of investment not in absolute terms but relative to the size of the increase in sales revenue. It is therefore 'unit-free'. This treatment of investment is appropriate because π and g, the other two variables involved, are also defined in such a way as to be unit-free.

In this form, the opportunity frontier specifies the maximum profit margin attainable given any particular growth rate of sales and any particular investment coefficient. In effect, it defines a subset of strategies each of which is dominant in the sense that no other strategy with the same (or a higher) growth rate and the same (or a lower) investment coefficient would yield a higher profit margin.

It follows from the discussion in the two subsections above that this function exhibits certain specific characteristics. First, given

---

* $\tilde{V}$ may be valued either at the prices of the preceding period (i.e. in money terms) or at the prices of the current period (i.e. in real terms). The substance of the argument does not depend on which of these two conventions is adopted. But see p. 106 below.

any particular value of the investment coefficient, the maximum attainable profit margin diminishes as the growth rate of sales increases (i.e. the partial derivative of the function with respect to g is negative). This is the demand–profit margin tradeoff; it reflects the fact that, once on the opportunity frontier, it is necessary for the firm to raise its unit selling costs and keep down its prices in order to increase the level of demand for its products in the face of competition from other firms. Secondly, given any particular value of the growth rate, the maximum attainable profit margin increases as the investment coefficient increases (i.e. the partial derivative of the function with respect to k is positive). This reflects the fact that, once the opportunity frontier has been attained, increasing the level of investment expenditure has a beneficial effect on the position of the demand–profit margin tradeoff, as a result, for example, of reductions in unit operating costs achieved by the replacement of older machinery. (Incidentally, it should be borne in mind that all these propositions refer to the opportunity frontier of a particular firm in a particular period, and not to comparisons between different firms and different periods.)*

A pedagogical advantage of representing the opportunity frontier in this way is that it makes explicit the double role of investment. (a) Its role in providing the additional capacity needed to supply increases in demand can be seen from the fact that the level of investment expenditure is determined by the extent of the growth in sales revenue, gV, in conjunction with the investment coefficient, k. That is, $I = k.gV$, which may be regarded as a simple unlagged version of the accelerator principle (this interpretation being clearest if we assume for simplicity that there is no initial excess capacity.) (b) The role of investment as an influence on the competitive efficiency of the firm, on the other hand, can be seen from the fact that the size of the investment coefficient affects the position of the demand–profit margin tradeoff.

* There is, for example, no presumption that in cross-section firms with high growth rates will have low profit margins. For different firms have different opportunity frontiers, and differences between firms (in, say, their growth rates) are likely to be attributable more to differences in the locations of their opportunity frontiers than to differences in their locations *on* their opportunity frontiers.

(iv) *The opportunity frontier further discussed*

Regardless of the way in which we choose to express it formally, the form of a company's opportunity frontier depends on the expectations of its managers with regard to a wide range of factors, of which the rate of aggregate economic growth, consumer behaviour, technology, input prices, market structure and the behaviour of competitors are the most prominent. The position of a firm's opportunity frontier also depends heavily on its history; for its opportunities in any given period will be conditioned to a very great extent by the nature of its inheritance of product lines, goodwill, equipment and manpower. Of equal importance is the character of its management; in particular, businessmen vary widely in their ability to notice and exploit opportunities. In consequence, different managers might well perceive different opportunity frontiers for the same firm.

Another reason why the form of a company's opportunity frontier is dependent on the nature of its management emerges when one considers the impact of uncertainty, an aspect of the opportunity set which has so far been neglected. For the choice between alternative strategies will be greatly influenced by the fact that different strategies involve different degrees and different kinds of uncertainty, not least about the future behaviour of customers and competitors. In effect, each strategy is associated not, as we have hitherto implied, with single-valued outcomes in terms of profit margin, sales growth and investment expenditure, but with sets of outcomes to which managers attach varying degrees of likelihood (or subjective probabilities).

It is simplest, and not too unreasonable, to assume that managers respond to uncertainty of this kind in something like the following way. (The simplification in question is in no sense fundamental to the present theory. It is doubtful, though, whether a more elaborate treatment of uncertainty would add much in the way of realism, and it would inevitably render the exposition more complicated.)

(a) They classify individual strategies as 'acceptable' or 'unacceptable' in terms of risk, thereby partitioning the set of available strategies into two subsets. An unacceptable strategy is one which is too risky in the sense that the expected benefits from pursuing it are too small in relation to the uncertainties involved. The criterion of acceptability depends on what managers construe as benefits or losses and on their attitudes towards risk-taking.*

(b) Once this partitioning of the opportunity set has been accomplished, we shall take it that managers (1) exclude unacceptable strategies from further consideration, (2) make no further distinctions in terms of risk among acceptable strategies and (3) make their subsequent choices among strategies simply in terms of the expected average values of the profit margin, the growth rate and the investment coefficient associated with each strategy. That is, we shall interpret the opportunity frontier as the frontier of the subset of acceptable strategies, and we shall interpret the function $\pi \leqslant \mu(g, k)$ as a relationship between the expected average values of the variables involved. Other things being equal, the less risk averse is a firm's management, the more favourable will be its opportunity frontier.

3.3 THE FINANCE FRONTIER

In this section we return to the question of the availability of finance for the firm's investment expenditures, and its dependence on the level of the firm's profits, a subject which was investigated at length in chapter 2. Specifically, drawing on the conclusions of that chapter, we shall construct a formal long run relationship which specifies the minimum level of profits needed to provide finance for any particular level of investment.

This we shall call the 'finance frontier', since it prevents the firm from undertaking any strategy which generates 'too small' an amount of profits in relation to the amount of investment involved. In principle, of course, the firm could operate within the finance frontier; that is, it could pursue a strategy which generated profits in excess of this minimum (for example, by accumulating more than the necessary minimum of financial assets). But in practice, for reasons that will become more apparent later, the firm will always choose a strategy which lies *on* the finance frontier.

* Incidentally, in partitioning the opportunity set, managers must bear in mind not only those characteristics of strategies which have been discussed in the present section but also the form of the finance frontier, which is discussed in the next section.

We shall construct a formal expression for the finance frontier in stages, dealing first with the determination of the financial asset ratio, second with the determination of the external finance ratio and third with the determination of the gross retention ratio. It should be stressed that in this section we are concerned exclusively with strategic behaviour; that is, the finance frontier (like the opportunity frontier) is a long run relationship. The role of short run finance policy will be considered separately towards the end of the chapter.

(i) *The financial asset ratio*

This, it may be recalled, is the ratio of the firm's acquisition of financial assets to its investment expenditure. For reasons connected with its short run finance policy, the firm will plan to hold, on average, a certain minimum proportion of its assets in liquid form. This minimum proportion (which we shall express as a ratio of financial to physical assets) is the 'target liquidity ratio'; its size is determined by the firm's expectations about the extent of future short run deficits on capital account in relation to the availability of short term credit facilities. Thus the minimum necessary acquisition of financial assets in any long period depends on the size of the firm's target liquidity ratio, on the extent of the increase in the value of its physical assets (which is equal to investment minus depreciation provisions plus any increase in the value of existing assets caused by inflation) and on the size of its initial stock of financial assets relative to its initial stock of physical assets.

We may therefore draw a simple diagram (figure 1) which relates the minimum necessary acquisition of financial assets (F) to the level of investment (I). Let us call the relationship $F(I)$ the 'financial asset frontier'; in order to achieve or exceed its liquidity target, the firm must be at a point on or above this frontier, in the region which is shaded in the diagram. The frontier has a constant positive slope because the minimum necessary acquisition of financial assets rises in proportion to investment, the proportion being determined by (a) the size of the target liquidity ratio and (b) the rate at which new investment depreciates or appreciates in value over the current period. The frontier does not in general pass through the origin, principally because the value

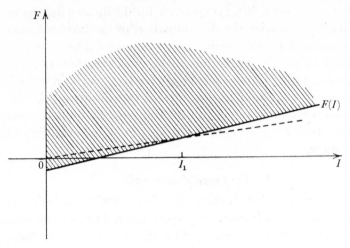

Figure 1

of existing physical assets does not in general remain constant over time.*

Since the target or minimum financial asset ratio, f, is defined as F/I, its value at any particular level of I can be represented by the slope of a ray from the origin through the relevant point on the financial asset frontier.† One such ray (corresponding to a specific value of I, I_1) is shown in the diagram as a broken line. Since the financial asset frontier does not in general pass through the origin, it is clear that the target value of the financial asset ratio is not in

* Algebraically, $F(I) = f'(1-\delta)\,(1+i)\,(I+K) - \tilde{F}$, where $f' =$ target liquidity ratio, $\delta =$ average rate of depreciation of physical assets at constant prices, $i =$ average rate of increase in prices of physical assets, $K =$ initial value of physical assets and $\tilde{F} =$ current value of initial stock of financial assets. The slope $\partial F/\partial I$ is $f'(1-\delta)\,(1+i)$ and the intercept of $F(I)$ is

$$f'(1-\delta)\,(1+i)\,K - \tilde{F},$$

which may be either positive or negative. It should be noted that in order to simplify the algebra we have ignored the possibility that I may depend on i because of the way in which investment in stocks is measured – see p. 11 above. In effect we have assumed (a) that investment in stocks is measured net of stock appreciation and (b) that the level of stocks is measured at current prices. These two assumptions conform more closely with those made by national accountants than with those made by company accountants under either 'first in, first out' or 'last in, first out' conventions.

† In other words, if the angle between the ray in question and the abscissa is θ, $f = \tan\theta$.

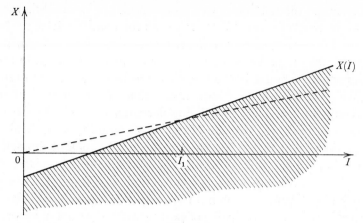

Figure 2

general a constant with respect to the level of investment. We ought therefore to write it as $f(I)$.*

(ii) *The external finance ratio*

This is the ratio of external finance (new borrowing and share issues) to investment. Because of the risks of borrowing, an upper limit is imposed by managers on the firm's gearing ratio (the ratio of debt to the total value of physical and financial assets). The size of this gearing limit depends on the interest rate, on the variability and uncertainty of the firm's future profits and on the degree of risk aversion among its managers. Thus the maximum possible amount of new borrowing in any long period is determined by the size of the gearing limit, by the initial level of outstanding debt and by the extent of the increase in the value of the firm's physical and financial assets (which depends on investment, depreciation, the liquidity ratio and changes in the value of existing assets caused by inflation). As a general rule, companies do not raise any finance by new issues of shares, principally because these are disliked by shareholders. However, new issues are made in exceptional circumstances, especially when a firm has a strong reason for undertaking a large off-trend burst of investment.

We may accordingly draw another simple diagram (figure 2)

---

* The function $f(I)$ is of the form $f = (1-\delta)(1+i)f' + \text{constant}/I$. That is, f tends asymptotically to $(1-\delta)(1+i)f'$.

which relates the maximum available amount of external finance (X) to the level of investment. Let us call the relationship $X(I)$ the 'external finance frontier'; in order to avoid exceeding its gearing limit, the firm must be at a point on or below this frontier, in the region which is shaded in the diagram. The frontier has a constant positive slope because new borrowing capacity rises in proportion to investment, the proportion being determined by (a) the size of the gearing limit, (b) the size of the target liquidity ratio (which affects the extent of the increase in the firm's stock of financial assets) and (c) the rate at which new investment depreciates or appreciates in value over the current period. This frontier, like the financial asset frontier, does not normally pass through the origin, again chiefly because the value of existing assets does not in general remain constant over time. A new issue of shares may be represented as an upward shift of the frontier, or, more exactly, as an increase in its intercept on the vertical axis.*

Since the target or maximum external finance ratio, x, is defined as X/I, its value at any particular level of I can be represented by the slope of a ray from the origin through the relevant point on the external finance frontier. Such a ray (corresponding to a specific value of I, I_1) is shown in the diagram as a broken line. Since the external finance frontier does not in general pass through the origin, the target value of the external finance ratio is not in general a constant with respect to the level of investment. We ought therefore to write it as $x(I)$.†

(iii) *The gross retention ratio*

This is the ratio of internal finance (depreciation provisions and retained earnings) to profits. Retained earnings are defined as pro-

---

* Algebraically, $\quad X(I) = \mathcal{N} + x'(1+f')\,(1-\delta)\,(1+i)\,(I+K) - \tilde{D},\quad$ where $\mathcal{N}$ = proceeds of new issues, x' = gearing limit and $\tilde{D}$ = initial value of outstanding debt. (The definitions of the other terms and a comment on the treatment of stocks are to be found in n* on p. 74 above.) The slope $\partial X/\partial I$ is

$$x'(1+f')\,(1-\delta)\,(1+i)$$

and the intercept of $X(I)$ is

$$\mathcal{N} + x'(1+f')\,(1-\delta)\,(1+i)\,K - \tilde{D},$$

which may be either positive or negative.

† The function $x(I)$ is of the form $x = x'(1+f')\,(1-\delta)\,(1+i) + \text{constant}/I$. That is, x tends asymptotically to $x'(1+f')\,(1-\delta)\,(1+i)$.

fits plus non-trading income minus depreciation provisions, interest payments, taxation and dividends.

The magnitude of depreciation provisions depends on the size and composition of the firm's inherited capital stock, on the level and composition of its current investment and on the depreciation rules applied by its accountants. The extent of the firm's non-trading income depends on the size of its stock of financial assets (and thus on its target liquidity ratio) and on the rate of return on its financial assets. The level of interest payments depends on the extent of the firm's outstanding borrowing (and thus on its gearing target) and on the constellation of interest rates payable on its debt. The amount of taxation paid depends on the level of taxable profits (which are calculated by adding non-trading income to profits and subtracting interest payments and depreciation allowances), on the tax rates and, under certain tax systems, on the level of dividends.

The level of dividends depends on the extent of the company's earnings (i.e. profits plus non-trading income minus depreciation provisions, interest and taxation) and on its target payout ratio. The size of the target payout ratio is determined ultimately by the preferences of shareholders with regard to liquidity and risk. There are, however, important reasons for maintaining a relatively constant payout ratio over time. In consequence, the size of the target payout ratio in any period is determined very largely by its size in previous periods. Nonetheless, the payout ratio may be altered to a limited extent in response to such pressures as a change in the system of company taxation.

By way of summary, we may draw another simple diagram (figure 3) relating the amount of internal finance available (R) to the level of profits (P). We shall call the relationship $R(P)$ the 'internal finance function'.* It has two distinct ranges:

(a) The first range covers situations in which the firm is (in an accounting sense) making a loss, that is, when its net profits (which we shall define as profits plus non-trading income minus deprecia-

---

* An alternative approach would be to regard $R(P)$ as a *frontier* (i.e. as specifying the *maximum* amount of internal finance which could be generated by a particular level of profits), on the grounds that it is easier to raise the payout ratio than to lower it. To adopt this alternative approach, however, would in no way alter the substance of the present model.

77

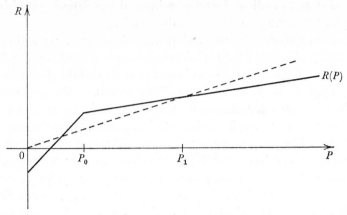

Figure 3

tion provisions and interest) are negative. In the diagram, this range lies to the left of the break-even level of profits, P_0. Since the firm is making a loss, we may assume that it pays neither taxes nor dividends. Over this range, then, the internal finance function has a slope of unity. Its intercept, which is normally negative, is equal to the amount of the firm's non-trading income minus its interest payments.

(b) The second range, which is the one that is relevant to the representative firm in the sort of economy with which we are concerned, covers those situations in which the firm's net profits are positive. In this range, the amount of internal finance available is equal to depreciation provisions minus interest payments plus non-trading income plus that fraction of net profits which remains after the payment of taxes and dividends. To the right of P_0 in the diagram, then, the internal finance function has a constant positive slope because internal finance increases in proportion to the level of profits, the proportion being determined by the tax rate and the payout ratio. In addition, the height of the function above the horizontal axis depends on the magnitude of depreciation provisions, non-trading income and interest payments (all of which depend to some extent on the level of investment).*

* An algebraic expression for $R(P)$ over the second range may be derived in stages as follows:

$$R = \text{DEPR} + \text{RETAINED EARNINGS}$$

78

Since the gross retention ratio, r, is defined as R/P, its value at any particular level of P can be represented in the diagram by the slope of a ray from the origin through the relevant point on the internal finance function. Such a ray (corresponding to a specific value of P, P_1) is shown in the diagram as a broken line. Since the internal finance function is not in general a straight line which passes through the origin, the gross retention ratio is not in general a constant with respect to the level of profits. Nor, because the height of the function above the horizontal axis depends on the level of investment, is the gross retention ratio a constant with respect to the level of investment. We ought therefore to write it as $r(P, I)$.*

(iv) *The finance frontier assembled from its components*

The financial asset ratio and the external finance ratio jointly determine the minimum amount of internal finance which would be needed in order to undertake any particular level of investment. For the minimum necessary total outlay on capital account would

where DEPR is the amount of depreciation provisions. Therefore

$$R = \text{DEPR} + (1 - \gamma)\,(1 - t)\,(P + \text{NTI} - \text{DEPR} - \text{INT}),$$

where γ is the payout ratio, t is (for simplicity) the ratio of tax payments to net profits, NTI is non-trading income and INT is interest payments. On the assumption that the liquidity ratio and the gearing ratio take on their target values, this expression can be developed further by making use of the three following relationships:

$$\text{DEPR} = \delta(1 + i)\,(I + K),$$

$$\text{NTI} = \bar{u}f'(1 - \delta)\,(1 + i)\,(I + K),$$

$$\text{INT} = ux'(1 + f')\,(1 - \delta)\,(1 + i)\,(I + K),$$

where $\bar{u}$ is the average rate of return on the company's financial assets and u is the average interest rate payable on its debt. (The other terms are defined in the footnotes on pp. 74 and 76 above.) After making the relevant substitutions and rearranging, one obtains the following expression for $R(P)$:

$$R = (1 - \gamma)\,(1 - t)\,P$$
$$+ (I + K)\,(1 + i)\,\{\delta + (1 - \gamma)\,(1 - t)\,[(\bar{u}f' - ux'(1 + f'))\,(1 - \delta) - \delta]\}.$$

The slope $\partial R/\partial P$ is $(1 - \gamma)\,(1 - t)$. The function is not homogeneous because the second term on the right-hand side of the above equation, which evidently depends on I, is in general non-zero – in practice, it is normally positive.

* The function $r(P, I)$ is of the form $r = (1 - \gamma)\,(1 - t) + (\text{function of } I)/P$.

be $(1+f)I$, and even if the firm were to raise the maximum possible amount of external finance, xI, the remainder of the outlay, $(1+f-x)I$, would have to be financed internally. In short, $R \geqslant (1+f-x)I$. The gross retention ratio in turn specifies the amount of internal finance that would be generated by any particular level of profits; that is $R = rP$. Between them, then, these three ratios determine the minimum level of profits that would be needed to finance any particular level of investment. For

$$rP \geqslant (1+f-x)I$$

and thus

$$P \geqslant \frac{(1+f-x)}{r}I,$$

which is the finance frontier.

As we have seen, f, x and r normally depend to some extent on I and P. Thus, strictly speaking, the finance frontier ought to be written as

$$P \geqslant \frac{(1+f(I)-x(I))}{r(P,I)}I.$$

But the essentials of the argument are in no way affected, and exposition is made much simpler, if we assume that the values taken on by f, x and r are completely independent of the values taken on by I and P. In diagrammatic terms, this amounts to assuming that the finance frontier is an upward-sloping straight line which passes through the origin.* A particular advantage of this simplifying assumption is that it enables us to write a compact expression for the finance frontier in terms of the profit *margin*, the growth rate of sales and the investment coefficient (being the variables in

* In mathematical language, the effect of this assumption is to make minimum P an increasing linear homogeneous function of I, even though, given the assumptions that we made above about $F(I)$, $X(I)$ and $R(P)$, it should be an increasing non-homogeneous function made up of two linear segments covering, respectively, the ranges $P < P_0$ and $P > P_0$ (P_0 being the break-even level of profits.) This can be demonstrated by substituting into the inequality $R \geqslant I+F-X$ the expressions for $F(I)$, $X(I)$ and $R(P)$ which were derived in the footnotes on pp. 74, 76 and 78 above, and rearranging. It is not in any fundamental sense necessary that the finance frontier should be linear, even in segments; in principle, almost any monotonically increasing function would serve equally well, although a non-linear function would complicate the exposition.

terms of which we described the opportunity frontier). The expression in question is*

$$\pi \geqslant \frac{(1+f-x)}{r}gk.$$

It specifies the minimum profit margin necessary to provide finance for any particular growth rate of sales, given any particular value of the investment coefficient. For explanatory purposes, this formulation of the finance frontier is extremely convenient. We shall make a great deal of use of it in what follows.

It is unlikely that the form of a company's finance frontier will be entirely independent of the form of its opportunity frontier. For example, an exceptional improvement in the opportunity frontier might affect the finance frontier by causing a new issue of shares or a reduction in the payout ratio. Similarly, the degree of risk aversion among managers influences both the position of a firm's opportunity frontier and its target gearing and liquidity ratios; in particular, other things being equal, a lower degree of risk aversion would result in a more favourable opportunity frontier, a higher gearing ratio and a lower liquidity ratio. To some extent, then, there is probably a tendency for a more favourable opportunity frontier to be associated with a more favourable finance frontier (in the sense of a smaller amount of profits being required to finance any particular level of investment). To introduce this sort of interdependence into our model would not pose any problem of principle.† But in practice it would appear that it is of a second order of importance. For the most part, therefore, in order to keep the exposition simple, we shall proceed as if the finance frontier and the opportunity frontier were strictly independent of one another.

* For the expression $P \geqslant (1+f-x)\,I/r$ can be divided through by sales revenue, V, to become $P/V \geqslant (1+f-x)\,I/rV$, which is $\pi \geqslant (1+f-x)\,gk/r$ because $\pi \equiv P/V$, $g \equiv (V-\tilde{V})/V$ and $k \equiv I/(V-\tilde{V})$.
† The way in which it would be done is discussed on p. 90 below; see especially the footnote. (Neoclassical models of the type discussed in chapter 1, section 2, may be regarded as embodying a special kind of interdependence between the opportunity frontier and the finance frontier. For in such a model the firm would select a strategy from the opportunity set and a financial asset ratio without regard to the availability of finance; x and r would then adjust passively to ensure that exactly the right amount of finance was available.)

3.4 THE LONG RUN PROFIT MARGIN
IN A STATIC CONTEXT

We are now in a position to assemble a complete model of the way in which the firm chooses its long run (or full capacity) profit margin. In this section we shall set out a simple version of the model in a framework which is static in the sense that it relates to behaviour within a single long (three to five year) period. We shall also assume throughout this section that the firm is in long run equilibrium in the sense that the profit margin which it chooses ex ante turns out to have been appropriate ex post. More precisely, we shall assume (a) that the firm accurately discerns the positions of its opportunity frontier and its finance frontier and (b) that stocks, the degree of capacity use, short term borrowing, financial asset holdings and the payout ratio are all at their target long run levels both at the beginning and at the end of the period. The model is made up of three elements, each of which, individually, has already been considered at some length. The elements in question are:

(1) The desire of those in charge of the firm to cause the largest possible increase in its sales revenue.

(2) The opportunity frontier, $\pi \leqslant \mu(g, k)$. This specifies the maximum profit margin attainable given any particular growth rate of sales and any particular investment coefficient. In effect, it defines a particular range of strategies, each of which is acceptable in terms of risk and yields a greater profit margin than any other acceptable strategy with the same growth rate and the same investment coefficient. It is convenient and not unreasonable to assume that the opportunity frontier is for all practical purposes continuous.*

(3) The finance frontier,

$$\pi \geqslant \frac{(1 + f - x)}{r} gk.$$

This specifies the minimum profit margin necessary to finance the

---

* Strict mathematical continuity would be an unreasonably strong assumption. In practice, however, strategies will be clustered sufficiently thickly along the frontier to render discontinuities negligibly small. This is because many of the detailed components of each strategy (prices, quantities of output, sales promotion expenditures, etc.) are in effect continuous variables.

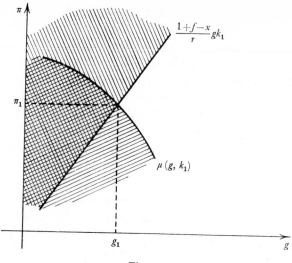

Figure 4

investment associated with any particular growth rate and any particular investment coefficient. We shall take it for granted that the finance frontier is effectively continuous.

It follows that a concise, but formal, way of stating the complete model is: (1) maximise g subject to two constraints, namely (2) $\pi \leqslant \mu(g, k)$ and (3)

$$\pi \geqslant \frac{(1 + f - x)}{r} gk.$$

These three requirements between them determine the firm's profit margin, π, the rate of growth of its sales, g, and its investment coefficient, k.

Having thus baldly stated the structure of the model, let us proceed to a fuller and less formal investigation of its properties and economic significance. In doing so, it is convenient to assume temporarily that the value of the investment coefficient is arbitrarily given. This transforms both the opportunity frontier and the finance frontier into relationships between two (rather than three) variables – the profit margin and the growth rate of sales – and enables us to expound the model with the aid of a simple diagram (figure 4).

Given a particular value (say k_1) for the investment coefficient, the opportunity frontier describes the dependence of the maximum attainable profit margin on the rate of growth of demand, this being what we called earlier the demand-profit margin tradeoff. Because the firm is engaged in a competitive struggle with other firms, it can increase the growth of demand for its products only by reducing its best attainable profit margin. The opportunity frontier is therefore represented in the diagram by a line (labelled $\mu(g, k_1)$) sloping down from left to right, beneath which lies a region (shaded in the diagram) containing 'accessible' strategies.

Correspondingly, given a particular value for the investment coefficient, the finance frontier specifies the minimum profit margin necessary to finance the capacity expansion required by any given growth rate of sales. The higher the growth rate, the greater the minimum necessary profit margin, because a faster rate of capacity expansion requires a higher ratio of investment expenditure to sales revenue. The finance frontier is therefore represented in the diagram by a line (labelled $[(1 + f - x)/r]\, gk_1$) sloping up from left to right, above which lies a region (shaded in the diagram) containing 'financially viable' strategies.

Between them, the opportunity frontier and the finance frontier define a limited subset of strategies, each of which is both 'accessible' and 'financially viable'. This subset is contained in the region which is cross-hatched in the diagram. The firm must choose a strategy which lies in this region (a strategy, that is, which satisfies both the opportunity constraint and the finance constraint). Furthermore, since the firm wishes to maximise its growth rate (i.e. to be as far to the right of the diagram as possible), it is immediately apparent from figure 4 that, from among the many alternatives in the subset in question, it will choose that strategy which is defined by the intersection of the opportunity frontier and the finance frontier (where the profit margin is π_1 and the growth rate is g_1). For it is a necessary condition for the maximisation of the growth rate of sales that the firm should be on both frontiers simultaneously, or, in other words, that both the opportunity constraint and the finance constraint should bind.*

* Hence the significance of our continuity assumptions (pp. 82–3 above). In particular, were the opportunity frontier discontinuous, maximisation of g would not necessarily entail the choice of a strategy on the finance frontier (i.e. the finance constraint would not necessarily bind). This would make virtually no difference to the substance of the model, but it would make the present method of exposition more complicated.

The economic interpretation of this condition (which must be satisfied whether or not the value of the investment coefficient is arbitrarily given) is straightforward. No growth-maximising firm will choose a strategy inside the opportunity frontier (that is, where the profit margin is less than the maximum attainable given any particular growth rate and investment coefficient) because one of the constraints on its expansion is the availability of finance which, at any given growth rate, could be increased by raising the profit margin. Likewise, no growth-maximising firm will choose a strategy inside the finance frontier (that is, where the profit margin is greater than the minimum necessary to finance any particular growth rate, given a particular investment coefficient) because one of the constraints on its expansion is demand which, given any particular investment coefficient, could be increased by reducing the profit margin. That is to say, the desire to maximise growth in the face of competition from other firms (i.e. to keep the profit margin as low as possible) drives the firm to acquire only the minimum necessary amount of financial assets and to make use of the maximum possible amount of external finance. (This, of course, is why we asserted earlier that the firm would (a) keep its actual liquidity ratio down to the target minimum and (b) push its actual gearing ratio up to the maximum imposed by its gearing limit.)

In each case, the firm has an incentive to be on one of the frontiers because of the existence of the other frontier. In consequence, we can forget about the regions within the opportunity frontier and the finance frontier. In formal terms, therefore, we can state that, if the growth rate is to be maximised, the profit margin must satisfy the two equations (as opposed to inequalities)

$$\pi = \mu(g, k)$$

and

$$\pi = \frac{(1 + f - x)}{r} gk.$$

These equations constitute two relationships between three unknown variables (π, g and k). If, in addition, one assumes (as we have temporarily done) that the value of k is arbitrarily given, the two equations uniquely determine the values of π and g.*

* The solution is unique because one equation is monotone increasing and the other is monotone decreasing. But see p. 89n below.

This additional assumption is valuable because it enables us to focus on what is perhaps the most important aspect of the profit margin decision. For when the value of the investment coefficient is given (i.e. when a fixed amount of investment expenditure is needed to provide a unit increase in capacity), it is clear from the diagram that the profit margin is the net outcome of two conflicting pressures, both of which arise from the desire of businessmen to maximise the growth of sales. One pressure, competition from other firms, tends to cause the choice of a low profit margin, because this increases the maximum attainable growth rate of demand. The other pressure, the need to make finance available for capacity expansion, tends to cause the choice of a high profit margin, because this increases the maximum financially viable growth rate of capacity. The profit margin ultimately chosen is that which strikes a balance between these two sorts of pressures in the sense that it makes the maximum attainable growth rate of demand equal to the maximum financially viable growth rate of capacity.

It is evident, however, that the level of the profit margin which achieves such a balance is itself dependent on the value of the investment coefficient, which affects both the firm's competitive efficiency and its financial needs. This can easily be illustrated in our diagram (see figure 5). Consider, for example, the consequences of a higher level of the investment coefficient (k_2) as a result, say, of the installation of more capital-intensive machinery or of a faster rate of replacement of existing machinery. (a) By reducing unit operating costs and thus increasing the maximum attainable profit margin at any given rate of growth of demand, a higher investment coefficient causes an upward shift of the demand–profit margin tradeoff (to a new position labelled $\mu(g, k_2)$ in the diagram). (b) It also increases the slope of the finance frontier (pushing it up to a new position labelled $[(1+f-x)/r]gk_2$ in the diagram), because a greater amount of investment is needed to provide any given amount of capacity and thus a higher minimum profit margin is needed to finance the capacity expansion entailed by any given growth rate of sales. The net result is that a different level of the profit margin is required in order to strike a balance between the maximum attainable growth rate of demand and the maximum financially viable growth rate of

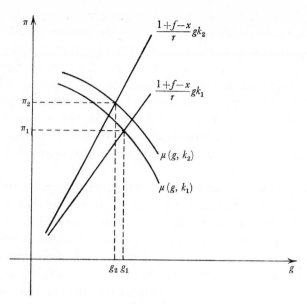

Figure 5

capacity. That is, the new value of the investment coefficient gives rise to a new pair of values for the profit margin and the growth rate (which are denoted in the diagram by π_2 and g_2 respectively).

Thus, given the form of the opportunity frontier and the form of the finance frontier, together with the assumption that the firm is seeking the greatest possible growth rate, any particular value of the investment coefficient will be associated both with the choice of a particular profit margin and with a particular rate of growth of sales. To complete our account of the way in which the profit margin is determined, we must evidently specify which of the various alternative values of the investment coefficient will be selected by the firm. The criterion is obvious; the firm will select that investment coefficient which is associated with the maximum rate of growth.

Let us examine the choice of the investment coefficient more closely by considering separately the two sorts of tendencies occasioned by, for example, a move to a higher level of the investment coefficient. (a) To begin with, let us artificially hold constant the position of the demand–profit margin tradeoff. The effect of an increase in the investment coefficient is therefore felt solely through the finance frontier, as an increase in the minimum profit margin necessary to finance any particular growth rate. This will tend, for obvious reasons, to cause the choice of a *higher* profit margin and a *lower* growth rate (as can be seen in figure 5). (b) Let us now artificially abstract from the effects of a higher investment coefficient on finance requirements and consider solely the consequences of a favourable shift in the demand–profit margin tradeoff. This will tend, again for obvious reasons, to cause the choice of a *higher* profit margin and a *higher* growth rate (as can be seen in figure 5).

When we combine the two sorts of tendencies which result from an increase in the investment coefficient, it is clear that a higher level of the investment coefficient will necessarily be associated with a higher level of the profit margin, since both tendencies pull in this direction. The effects of a higher level of the investment coefficient on the growth rate, however, are ambiguous, since the two tendencies pull in opposite directions; the outcome depends on their relative strengths. If, for example, the improvement in the demand–profit margin tradeoff is large relative to the increase in finance requirements, the net result will be a higher growth rate. If, however, the improvement in the demand-profit margin tradeoff is relatively small (as is the case in figure 5), the net result will be a lower growth rate.

It is plausible to assume that the opportunity frontier exhibits diminishing returns with respect to the investment coefficient, that is, that as the investment coefficient increases, further increases have progressively smaller beneficial effects on the position of the demand–profit margin tradeoff.* (One reason for this might be that the replacement of more and more recent vintages of machines yields smaller and smaller savings in unit operating costs, while the investment expenditure involved in replacing a machine is the same, whatever its vintage.) The increase in finance requirements caused by a rise in the investment coefficient, however, is constant at all levels of the investment coefficient; a doubling of the investment coefficient will always double the minimum profit margin necessary to finance any given growth

---

* It should be stressed that we refer here to diminishing returns with respect to the substitution of one input for another, and *not* to diminishing returns to scale.

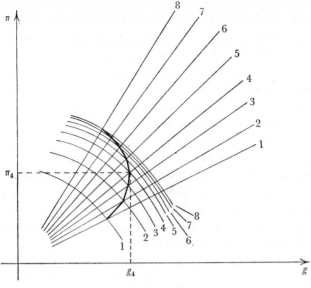

Figure 6

rate. In consequence, it is reasonable to suppose that, commencing at the lowest possible value of the investment coefficient, the net effect of increasing the investment coefficient is initially to raise the growth rate, but that as the level of the investment coefficient increases, the net effect of further increases is eventually to diminish the growth rate. At some intermediate level, therefore, there will be a watershed, where the growth rate attains its maximum, and it is this level of the investment coefficient which the growth-maximising firm will select.*

The way in which the firm chooses its investment coefficient can be illustrated by extending our earlier diagrams. Figure 6, for example, shows the demand–profit margin tradeoffs and the

* It is possible that more than one value of k, and hence more than one value of π, will be associated with maximum g. To this extent, the model will be indeterminate. Maximum g, incidentally, need not be positive; within certain limits, the principles of the present model apply also to shrinking firms. To incorporate this possibility, however, we would need (among other things) to take proper account of the non-homogeneity of the finance frontier, especially in the range in which profits are below the breakeven level (see n * on p. 80 above). Evidently, the model breaks down when the profit margin associated with maximum g is negative or so low as to cause the firm to close down.

finance frontiers corresponding to eight different values of the investment coefficient. The values of the profit margin and the growth rate associated with each value of the investment coefficient are connected by a heavy line. As the investment coefficient increases from k_1 to k_4, the growth rate rises. As the investment coefficient increases beyond k_4, the growth rate falls. The maximum value of the growth rate is attained at k_4, which is the investment coefficient that the firm will select. The chosen level of the profit margin will therefore be π_4.

It may be noted in passing that the principles according to which the investment coefficient is determined in the present model are similar to the orthodox theory of the choice of technique by a cost-minimising firm, in that what is involved in both cases, broadly speaking, is the choice of an optimal point on a tradeoff between low operating costs and low capital costs. But the present theory differs from the orthodox analysis with regard to the way in which capital costs are evaluated. In the orthodox theory, capital costs consist of depreciation charges plus some exogenously given 'target rate of return' on capital employed. In the present model, by contrast, although an implicit 'target rate of return' is involved, it is endogenously determined in an unorthodox way. This last proposition in particular, and the subject of the investment coefficient in general, will be discussed further at several points below (see especially pp. 98 and 120–1).

This concludes the exposition of the static equilibrium version of our model of the determination of the profit margin of the individual firm. At the beginning of this section it was asserted without proof that the drive to maximise growth, the opportunity frontier and the finance frontier between them determine not only the profit margin but also the growth rate and the investment coefficient. It has now been shown how this comes about.

At this point, let us very briefly relax our assumption that the form of the finance frontier is strictly independent of the form of the opportunity frontier.* In particular let us consider the possi-

---

* Formally, let $\mathbf{m}$ be a vector of parameters of the opportunity frontier. One may then write f, x and r as functions of $\mathbf{m}$, that is, as $f(\mathbf{m})$, $x(\mathbf{m})$ and $r(\mathbf{m})$. The complete model then becomes (1) maximise g, subject to (2) $\pi \leqslant \mu(g, k, \mathbf{m})$ and to (3) $\pi \geqslant (1 + f(\mathbf{m}) - x(\mathbf{m})) gk/r(\mathbf{m})$, which, as before, determines the values of π, g and k.

bility that an exceptionally favourable opportunity frontier, by increasing the external finance ratio or the gross retention ratio, might result in a more favourable finance frontier. This would clearly affect the firm's choice of strategy. Most notably, it would result in the choice of a profit margin which was lower (and a growth rate which was higher) than would otherwise have been the case.*

Finally, by way of a digression, a little more may be said about conflicts of interest between managers and shareholders. In chapter 2 we argued that the two groups have a great deal in common, despite the possibility of conflict over certain issues. This view can now be restated more precisely. The position of the opportunity frontier is, roughly speaking, an area of common interest.† Both managers and shareholders stand to gain from improvements in the company's selling and cost efficiency, managers because this increases the maximum attainable growth rate, and shareholders because this increases the company's profitability.

Conflicts of interest, on the other hand, arise mainly in connection with the choice of a position *on* the opportunity frontier. In the present model this depends on two things: (a) the form of the finance frontier, (b) the fact that managers wish to achieve the maximum possible growth rate. In chapter 2 we identified certain possible conflicts between managers and shareholders over the form of the finance frontier, in particular with regard to dividend policy and new issues of shares. We can now see that growth maximisation is a further area of conflict. For there is no reason to suppose that shareholders will in general derive greatest benefit from the pursuit of maximum sales growth.

Nonetheless, in practice the conflicts between managers and shareholders are of secondary importance in relation to the extent of their common interests, especially since the ability and

---

* Whether k is higher or lower than would otherwise have been the case will depend on the exact form of the opportunity frontier and on the extent of the change in the finance frontier.

† This statement requires qualification in two respects. First, managers and shareholders may differ over what should be the criterion of 'acceptability' in terms of risk; see pp. 71–2 above. Second, in certain cases a firm which was trying to maximise the present value of earnings rather than its growth rate might choose a strategy which lay *within* the opportunity frontier.

4-2

behaviour of a firm's managers have a great influence on the form of its opportunity frontier. It is of course true that managers who choose (from the shareholders' viewpoint) the 'wrong' position on the opportunity frontier could benefit their shareholders by a change of strategy. But if the firm in question has a favourable opportunity frontier, its shareholders may anyway be better off than those of another firm, with a less favourable opportunity frontier, whose managers have chosen the 'right' strategy. And if in some way a company's managers are disciplined as a result of the disapproval of its shareholders, it is more likely to be the penalty for inefficiency of various kinds than for choosing the wrong point on the opportunity frontier.

3.5 THE LONG RUN PROFIT MARGIN IN A DYNAMIC CONTEXT

In the preceding section, in order to simplify the exposition, we restricted our attention to behaviour within a single long period and we assumed that the firm was in equilibrium in the sense that its expectations of the future were fulfilled. But the principles embodied in the static model are of general relevance, and the purpose of the present section is to place them in a dynamic context characterised by a certain amount of disequilibrium. We shall not go about this by constructing a formal dynamic model, since this would be very difficult to do in any illuminating way.* Instead, we shall offer an informal dynamic interpretation of the static model.

The relevance of the static model to reality can best be seen if we adopt as our dynamic context a series of overlapping long periods.† Let us assume, for example, that the firm has a planning

* For example, although the static model could be transformed into a steady state growth model without any modification of the equations involved, such a transformation would, if anything, reduce the degree of realism. To incorporate the principles of the present theory in a system of difference equations, on the other hand, while it would increase the degree of realism, would be an extremely complicated exercise.

† We will retain two simplifying assumptions with respect to time: (a) The time horizon is assumed to be uniform for all the firm's activities; we neglect the possibility that the firm may plan further into the future on some fronts than on others. (b) We ignore the passage of time within the planning

horizon of five years and that it makes a long run plan every year. That is, the firm plans in 1975 for the years 1975–80, in 1976 for the years 1976–81, in 1977 for the years 1977–82, and so on. Each year, then, the managers of the firm decide on a target profit margin for the five year period ahead. The static model may be regarded as a description of the way in which this decision is made. In certain respects, however, the annual planning exercise is more complicated than the discussion in the last section would suggest. In particular, it involves not only the extension of the planning horizon further into the future and the development of policy to cover a period untouched by earlier plans, but also the updating and modification of plans made in earlier years on the basis of fresh information generated by the events of the past year. The latter aspect is significant because it is likely that some of this fresh information will reveal that the expectations entertained by the firm in earlier years were incorrect and thus that the firm is in disequilibrium in the sense of having chosen policies which now seem to its managers to be inappropriate. This, of course, will have an effect on the choice of policies in the current period.

Before proceeding further, it is important to establish that we are here concerned specifically with long run disequilibrium. For a firm may correctly anticipate developments over the long run while failing to predict their exact timing in the short run. Failures of this sort also call for adjustments of various kinds (with which we shall deal in the last section of this chapter). But for the time being we shall disregard them except in so far as they lead the firm to conclude that it is in long run disequilibrium.

Thus, since it is probable that the firm's expectations will often be to some extent confounded, it is necessary, in order to provide a proper description of the annual planning exercise, to supplement the static model with an account of the way in which the firm responds in the face of disequilibrium. However, given the principles according to which the profit margin is determined in a static context, it is usually not difficult to envisage how the firm

period, assuming, for instance, that the firm will plan to maintain a constant profit margin over the period and that profits at the beginning of the period are interchangeable with profits at the end of the period. Both these assumptions could be relaxed without affecting the essential principles of the argument.

would react to any specified type of disequilibrium. Let us consider three examples.

(a) The firm might wrongly predict the capital costs of its investment projects. For example, in a particular year it might realise that in an earlier period it had underestimated the cost of a projected expansion of production facilities. In consequence, although it had correctly planned the growth of its capacity in line with the growth of demand, its profits will not be large enough to pay for the necessary investment without reducing its stock of liquid assets below (or raising its borrowing above) the target long run level. In order to move back towards equilibrium, the firm must reduce its rate of expansion below what it would otherwise have been. It must increase its target profit margin by raising prices or cutting selling costs, which will reduce the growth of demand, and it must cut back on its investment in capacity expansion.

(b) To take a less gloomy instance, the firm might overestimate its operating and selling costs, and find itself faced with (either the reality or the prospect of) an unexpectedly high profit margin at its chosen price and output levels. This would tend to cause an accumulation of financial assets above the target long run level. In this situation the firm is clearly not making the most of its opportunities to expand its sales. It will therefore reduce its target profit margin (by lowering prices or increasing selling costs) with a view to stimulating additional demand, and at the same time it will increase its investment in capacity expansion.

(c) Consider finally a situation in which, although the firm correctly forecasts its profit margin, it wrongly predicts the actions of its customers and competitors and thus miscalculates the size of the increase in the demand for its products at its target profit margin. Let us label firms as 'pessimistic' or 'optimistic' according to whether the increase in demand exceeds or falls short of their expectations. A pessimistic firm, although its profits will be adequate to finance its planned investment, will have deficient capacity and will be failing to realise its full potential for growth. It will adjust by raising its target profit margin and increasing its investment in capacity expansion. Conversely, an optimistic firm will have excess capacity, and its realised profits will be insufficient to finance its investment without running down its liquid assets or building up excessive debt. It will respond by reducing its target profit margin in order to boost demand, and by cutting back its capacity expansion programme into line with what it now regards as the probable rate of growth of demand.

It is clear that in these examples of disequilibrium (all of which arise from misconceptions of the form of the opportunity frontier), we observe exactly the same forces acting on the profit margin that were described above in the context of the static equilibrium model. The desire to maximise the growth of sales emerges in all three examples. In addition, (1) the examples of excess capacity and of an unexpectedly high profit margin illustrate the downward pressure on the profit margin which is exerted by competition from other firms, while (2) the examples of deficient capacity and of unexpectedly high capital costs illustrate the upward pressure exerted on the profit margin by the need to generate finance for investment. And in a situation of disequilibrium, as in the context of the static model, the profit margin is chosen with a view to balancing these two conflicting pressures in such a way as to make the maximum attainable growth rate of demand equal to the maximum financially viable growth rate of capacity.

The substance of this section so far may be summarised as follows: the firm's current activities are always based on target policies which cover a period of several years ahead, but at comparatively short intervals, in the light of informational feedback from its current activities, it reviews and, where necessary, alters its long run targets, at the same time as making adjustments towards them in the face of disequilibrium. Each year, in our example, a new five year plan is drawn up, which is itself the subject of modification one year later. The word 'modification' should perhaps be stressed, since what is undertaken each year is not the development of new long run policy from scratch but the updating and extension of existing policy. Annually, in our example, the firm must decide whether the previously established target profit margin should be altered and, if so, in what direction and by how much.

This account of business behaviour in a dynamic context is by no means unrealistic (cf. Lintner, 1971, pp. 172–6). Moreover, the static model, though not a literal representation of this process, provides the basis of a description of the annual planning exercise and suggests the principles according to which the firm makes adjustments in situations of disequilibrium. Its adequacy as a *direct* description of reality depends largely on the proximity of the representative firm to long run equilibrium. More precisely, it depends on how close, in the long run, stocks, the degree of capacity use, short term borrowing, financial asset holdings and the payout ratio are to their target levels.

For the static model to be of value as a direct description of reality, it is not, of course, necessary to suppose that the firm ever attains equilibrium, let alone that it is continuously in equilibrium. What is necessary is that its adjustments in response to disequilibrium should be such as to prevent it from wandering too far away from equilibrium. For if the firm is normally a long way from equilibrium, the static model in itself becomes much less helpful as a way of accounting for the behaviour of the target profit margin. An explanation in terms of the principles of the present theory can still be provided, but it must focus on the far more complicated processes of adjustment, following the firm's changes of expectations and policies as it endeavours to move towards targets which are always too far away to be of practical relevance in themselves.

How close firms 'normally' are to equilibrium (in the respects with which the present theory deals) is a question to which it is hard to give a general answer. The discussion of disequilibrium above suggests that the model of the individual firm is stable in the sense that the firm will always adjust towards equilibrium, or, more accurately, in the sense that we have not introduced any considerations which might cause it to adjust away from equilibrium. How close the individual firm normally is to equilibrium thus depends on how good it is at forecasting, how promptly it responds to disequilibrium and how accurately it gauges the extent (as distinct from the direction) of the necessary response. The fact that adjustments entail costs (and that large adjustments entail large costs) suggests that firms will try to avoid frequent drastic adjustments and oscillatory over-shooting.

Hence, from a narrowly microeconomic (or partial equilibrium) point of view, closeness to long run equilibrium is a function of managerial competence tempered by chance, and it is probably reasonable to suppose that the static model normally provides an acceptable description of the way in which the profit margin of the 'representative' firm is determined in any particular three to five year period. (A corollary of this is that the calculation of three to five year moving averages of the profit margin and of the other variables with which the model deals would normally provide acceptable estimates of their long run target or equilibrium values.) Naturally, from a macroeconomic viewpoint we must acknowledge the possibility that firms in aggregate may respond to disequilibrium in such a way as to make matters worse. But, as it happens, the discussion of aggregate instability which we shall undertake in the next chapter will not lead us to abandon the point of view adopted in the present paragraph.

It is of some interest, by way of a conclusion to this section, to say a little about 'yield' calculations and their role in company investment decisions. We shall define a yield calculation as any estimate of the expected 'rate of return' on an investment project (i.e. the increase in the firm's profits as a result of undertaking the project expressed as some sort of ratio of the investment outlay involved). It is quite common for firms to make such estimates, albeit in a variety of ways (see, for example, NEDC, 1965; Neild, 1964; Williams and Scott, 1965; Barna, 1962; and *The Director*, 1970). The most widely employed measures of yield are the payoff period and its close relation the gross accounting rate of return – there are also a handful of other measures in use, including a number of discounted cash flow techniques.* Anyway, once the

---

* The payoff period is the length of time which elapses before the accumulated gross profits of a project equal the investment outlay involved. The gross accounting rate of return is some measure of the (annual) gross profits generated by a project as a ratio of the investment outlay involved. If the profits of a project are constant in each year of its life, the payoff period is the reciprocal of the gross accounting rate of return. For a fuller discussion of these and other measures of yield, see (in addition to the references cited in the text) Merrett and Sykes (1966); their discussion, unlike the present discussion, is set in a neoclassical context. (The reason for classifying Merrett and Sykes as neoclassical is *not* that they advocate the use of discounted cash flow techniques, whose advantages apply also to the type of firm discussed in the present chapter. It is, rather, that they tend to assume (a) that firms are present value maximisers, for whom a necessary and sufficient condition for undertaking an investment project is that its expected yield should exceed some externally given 'interest rate' and (b) that, provided this condition is fulfilled, firms will have no difficulty in obtaining the necessary finance from one source or another.)

expected yield on a project has been calculated by one or other of these methods, the firm compares it with some target yield, and the comparison is used as a guide in deciding whether or not to undertake the project.

In the present model, it will be recalled, firms choose among alternative courses of action by asking (a) are particular strategies in the opportunity set financially viable (that is, could the investment which they involve be financed) and (b) to what extent would they increase sales. In this context, yield calculations provide a rough and ready means of assessing the financial viability of individual investment projects. They are of particular relevance to the choice of the investment coefficient, that is, in connection with replacement decisions and decisions between alternative ways of providing given amounts of capacity. More generally, yield calculations are useful in circumstances in which (a) alternative investment projects must be assessed sequentially rather than simultaneously or (b) it is desired to decentralise the investment decision-making process within the firm.

The significance of yield calculations in the context of the present model can best be exposed by expressing the finance frontier as a constraint not on the firm's profit margin, but on its profit *rate*. This could be done in various alternative ways, employing different definitions of the profit rate. The simplest is to rewrite the finance frontier in the form

$$\rho \geqslant \frac{(1+f-x)}{r}(g_K+\delta)$$

where ρ = the profit rate (defined in this instance as the ratio of profits to the book value of physical assets at current prices); g_K = the real rate of growth (i.e. the rate of growth at constant prices) of the firm's stock of physical assets, net of depreciation – if the physical capital–output ratio were to remain constant over time, this would be equal to the rate of growth of the volume of the firm's sales; and δ = the average rate of depreciation of physical assets at constant prices.*

* This expression is derived by dividing the original expression for the finance frontier, $P \geqslant (1+f-x) I/r$, by the book value of physical assets at current prices, $\overline{K}$, to obtain $P/\overline{K} \geqslant (1+f-x) I/r\overline{K}$. By definition, $P/\overline{K} = \rho$ and $I/\overline{K} = g_K+\delta+\lambda$, where λ is the ratio of stock appreciation to $\overline{K}$ (see p. in

In its revised form, the finance frontier specifies that the firm's average profit rate must exceed some minimum, which we will label $\hat{\rho}$. The size of this minimum profit rate depends on, among other things, the firm's growth rate; in particular, it is clear that the higher is g_K, the higher will be $\hat{\rho}$.

Let us interpret $\hat{\rho}$ as the firm's target yield (or target rate of return). Comparison of the estimated yield on a particular project (which we shall label ρ_i) with the target gives an indication of the project's financial viability. If ρ_i is greater than $\hat{\rho}$, the project would not only 'pay for itself' but would generate a 'surplus'. If, on the other hand, ρ_i is less than $\hat{\rho}$, the project would need to be 'subsidised' out of the surplus generated by projects earning more than the target yield. In deciding whether or not to undertake a particular project, the firm will accordingly weigh the comparison of its expected yield with the target yield against the attractiveness of the project in terms of its direct contribution to sales growth. For example, the firm might be willing to 'subsidise' capacity expansion projects, but not replacement projects.

This procedure, non-rigorous as it may appear, resembles quite closely the way in which firms actually use yield calculations (see especially Williams and Scott, 1965, chs. 6 and 7; Barna, 1962, ch. 3; Carter and Williams, 1958; National Association of Accountants, 1964). It does not, of course, depend on the employment of any particular measure of yield. The example above is in effect couched in terms of the gross accounting rate of return (a measure which is more or less equivalent to the payoff period). But exactly the same principles would apply were the firm, say, to calculate present values by discounting the net cash flows of individual projects at the target rate of profit (although this would require the target rate to be defined net of depreciation and taxation).

There is one respect, though, in which matters are more complicated than we have so far admitted. For it is clear from our expression for the finance frontier that the firm must know its

above). In order to simplify the algebra, let us assume in this context that company accountants measure investment in stocks net of stock appreciation and thus that λ is always zero. In reality, given the widespread use of the 'first in, first out' convention for valuing stocks, changes in the general price level affect the amount of finance required for working capital and thus λ is an additional influence on the target yield whose size depends on the rate of inflation.

growth rate before it can know its target rate of return, and, strictly speaking, it cannot know g_K *until* it knows $\hat{\rho}$ (since the growth rate will depend on what investment projects the firm decides to undertake). In practice, therefore, the firm may well use some iterative approach. For example, it may begin by using its past profit rate as the target, and then raise the target if the initial figure appears to lead to an excess of acceptable projects over available funds or reduce it if it appears to lead to an excess of funds over projects. Indeed, such modifications may form part of the annual update of the long run plan: the recognition that earlier decisions were based on too high or too low a target yield will lead to the adoption of a lower or a higher target in the current round of planning.

3.6 THE LONG RUN AND THE SHORT RUN

Up to this point the discussion in the present chapter has been confined exclusively to the long run. Our principal object has been to provide an explanation of the size of the long run profit margin, being the margin over unit costs at normal full capacity use. In this final section we shall address ourselves briefly to the short run, in which, as we shall show, the pattern of causation is rather different.

We have defined long run equilibrium as a situation in which, in the long run, stocks, the degree of capacity use, short term borrowing, financial asset holdings and the payout ratio are all at their long run target levels. We have also considered situations of long run disequilibrium in which, in the long run, these equilibrium conditions are not fulfilled. In such circumstances, as we have seen, the firm will adjust its long run policies with a view to restoring equilibrium.

However, even in long run equilibrium it is highly improbable that these conditions will be fulfilled in any particular short period. More specifically, what is necessary for long run equilibrium is that these conditions should be fulfilled over the planning period as a whole, not in any particular sub-period. Thus the firm will tolerate their nonfulfillment, and will make no adjustments to its long run policies, as long as it believes this to be a temporary (or short run) state of affairs in the sense that, over the planning period as a whole, discrepancies in one direction will average out with discrepancies in the other direction.

Such temporary discrepancies may arise from many causes. Some of them may be accurately anticipated by the firm. For example, it would be expensive and inefficient to match investment outlays to the availability of retained profits on a month-by-month or year-by-year basis, even if it were possible to predict both of them with certainty. Thus although the firm will aim to make its retained profits equal to some specific proportion of its investment over the planning period as a whole, it will also allow for surpluses and shortfalls in particular sub-periods, which will be absorbed by deviations of liquid asset holdings and short term borrowing around their long run target levels. Similarly, although the firm will plan to keep demand and capacity in line with one another in the long run, it would be expensive if not impossible to preserve the long run target relationship between them in each sub-period, even if they could be very accurately forecast. The firm will therefore plan to install capacity ahead of demand in certain sub-periods and to allow demand to exceed capacity in others, thereby causing short run deviations of stocks and capacity utilisation around their long run target levels.

Of greater interest in some respects are *unanticipated* short run discrepancies. Not least, demand fluctuates in the short run in an erratic way. Inevitably, week by week and month by month, sales are not made at a steady rate, and on top of this, year-to-year fluctuations in demand are caused by short term oscillations in the level of aggregate economic activity. Likewise, the availability of capacity varies in the short run, due to strikes, breakdowns, shortages of materials and so forth. Moreover, the time pattern of current expenditures cannot be foreseen with certainty. Singly and in combination, these factors give rise to unpredictable short run variations in profits. In addition, it is common for there to be unforeseeable changes in the time pattern of investment outlays.

Circumstances in which these sorts of unanticipated discrepancies exist might be described as 'short run disequilibria'. But short run disequilibrium is perfectly compatible with long run equilibrium. For provided the discrepancies in question are believed by the firm to be of a temporary nature, they will have no effect on its long run expectations and in consequence will cause no changes in its long run policies. Specifically, (a) the target profit margin, (b) investment expenditure and (c) dividends will all be maintained, as far as is possible, at their chosen long run levels.

As a result of the maintenance of long run policies in the face of short run disequilibrium, stocks, the degree of capacity use, short term borrowing, financial asset holdings and the payout ratio will all fluctuate capriciously in the short run around their long run target levels. Consider, for instance, the effects of an unexpected temporary fall in demand. This would initially cause a rise in stocks (which in itself would require an increase in short term borrowing or a reduction of liquid asset holdings). Moreover, if the reduction in demand were to exceed some critical size, it would cause a reduction in output and in the degree of capacity use, which would cause a fall in the absolute level of profits. The desire to stabilise dividends (which would cause a temporary rise in the payout ratio), together with the need to meet fixed interest payments, would cause a proportionally greater fall in the availability of internal finance. This in turn would cause a reduction of financial asset holdings or an increase in short term borrowing, since the firm would keep up its planned long run investment programme by selling securities or obtaining additional bank loans.

There are, of course, limits on the extent to which the firm can, in effect, ignore short run disequilibrium. For example, the firm's ability to adjust to a temporary excess of demand is limited both by the size of its stocks and by the degree to which capacity utilisation can be raised above normal (by overtime, shiftwork and so forth); beyond a certain point, supply cannot be increased and the firm's customers must queue or go elsewhere. Similarly, there are limits on the firm's ability to carry out its investment programme in the event of a short run decline in profits; even if it believes this decline to be a temporary state of affairs, it may exhaust its liquid assets and credit facilities and be forced to postpone some investment expenditure, particularly on replacement and modernisation projects. (Indeed, this is the way in which government-induced credit squeezes directly affect industrial investment.) It follows that short run increases in demand and profits (and in the availability of credit) may sometimes directly stimulate investment by providing the liquidity necessary to carry out projects that had been postponed earlier. Furthermore, it should be emphasised that in practice the distinction between the long run and the short run is blurred. That is to say, firms tend to interpret actual deviations from target stock, capacity use and liquidity levels as symptoms partly of short run disequilibrium and partly of long run disequilibrium. In consequence, such deviations will normally lead to a certain amount of alteration of long run policies in addition to the specifically short run responses described above.

The long run profit margin is unaffected by short run disequilibrium as such. However, for reasons of a familiar kind, the actual profit margin (i.e. the ratio of profits to sales revenue) in any short period is affected by deviations both of stocks and of the degree of capacity use from their long run target levels.

(a) It is affected by fluctuations in stocks because profits are by definition equal to sales revenue minus operating costs, where operating costs are defined as current outlays minus increases in stocks. Thus, for example, a reduction in sales at a constant level of output would cause no change in the absolute level of profits since stocks would rise (and hence operating costs would fall) by exactly the amount that sales had fallen. It would, however, raise the ratio of profits to sales revenue (although the ratio of profits to output would be unaltered).

(b) The actual profit margin is affected by changes in the degree of capacity use because of the existence of overhead costs of various sorts, which cause short run variations in costs to be proportionally smaller than short run variations in output. Not least, recent studies have suggested that labour of all types is treated by firms as an overhead in the short run.* Consider, for example, a reduction in output induced by what is regarded as a temporary decrease in demand. Because there are moral, social and economic costs to firing and rehiring labour, workers are laid off less than in proportion to the reduction in output, even after overtime working has been reduced. The wage and salary bill therefore falls proportionally less than the value of output, and the ratio of profits to output declines. This tends to depress the ratio of profits to sales.

* See Neild (1963) and Solow (1968). It may be noted that Neild remarks (on p. 5) that 'in brief, it is implied that prices are generally set in relation to wages by long run considerations'. The present theory of the long run profit margin is, of course, an attempt to explain what those considerations actually are.

For both these reasons, which tend in practice to offset one another to some extent, the firm's actual profit margin is bound to fluctuate erratically in the short run around its long run target level. If the firm is in long run equilibrium, these short run fluctuations cancel out and the average actual profit margin over the planning period as a whole is equal to the long run target profit margin.

4

THE SHARE OF PROFITS IN
NATIONAL INCOME

4.1 PROFITS, COMPETITION AND GROWTH

In this chapter we shall develop and discuss a theory of the determination of the share of profits in national income in the long run. In essence, the theory is simply an extension of the model of the determination of the profit margin of the individual firm which was put forward in the preceding chapter. In other words, the main purpose of the present chapter is to transplant the principles of our microeconomic model into a macroeconomic framework.

Let us begin by redefining the variables of the microeconomic model in such a way that they apply to the company sector as a whole (provisionally assuming for convenience that there are no multinational companies).* In the case of absolute variables (such as P and I), this involves no more than simple addition across all the firms of which the company sector is composed. In the case of those variables which are ratios (most notably π, f, x, r, g and k), it involves calculating weighted averages across all companies. For example, the company sector profit margin is a weighted average of the profit margins of all individual companies, the relevant weights being their shares of total company sector sales, while the external finance ratio of the company sector is a weighted average of the external finance ratios of all individual companies, the relevant weights being their shares of total company sector investment. From this point onwards, then, and without making any changes in the notation, we shall interpret all variables as relating to the company sector as a whole. It is worth making four general comments at this stage.

---

* This assumption is relaxed on pp. 148–54 below. Given this assumption (which implies, inter alia, that net foreign investment by companies is zero), $(f-x)I$ is the net acquisition of financial assets by industrial and commercial companies, in the sense in which this phrase is used in the British national accounts; see n * on p. 1 above.

(1) The values taken on by those aggregate variables which are ratios depend not only on the values of the corresponding variables of individual firms but also on the weights which are attached to them, which reflect, roughly speaking, the relative sizes of individual firms. Much the same is true of absolute variables; large firms have a greater effect than small firms on the behaviour of the aggregates. In this way, and in other ways, the microeconomic or structural factors which govern relative prices and quantities inevitably exert an influence on macroeconomic phenomena such as the share of profits in national income. But we shall simplify our macroeconomic model in the traditional manner, by assuming for the most part that the microeconomic structure of the economy is exogenously determined in the sense that it is unaffected by changes in the aggregate variables with which the model deals. Strictly speaking, this is not a legitimate assumption; for example, changes in the share of profits might well alter the relative sizes of individual firms by affecting the commodity composition of output. However, in the context of the present model, it is not unreasonable to suppose that interdependence of this kind is in practice of a second order of importance.

(2) It is unlikely that the time periods relevant to individual firms (especially for planning purposes) will all be of the same length. Nor, even where they are of the same length, will they necessarily be synchronised with one another. For this reason, causal or behavioural statements about aggregate variables inevitably do a certain amount of violence to reality. This problem is common to all macroeconomic theories.

(3) It is also worth noting at the outset that the aggregate growth rate, g, can be defined either in real terms or in money terms without affecting the substance of the argument, provided that the investment coefficient, k, is defined in a consistent way. For it is clear from the definitions of g and k (p. 69) that the value of their product, gk, which is central to the present theory, does not depend on which of these two conventions is adopted. For convenience, we shall assume throughout that g is measured in real terms; k will accordingly be defined as the ratio of investment (valued at current prices) to the absolute increase in the volume of sales (valued at current prices).

(4) At the same time, but quite separately (i.e. regardless of

whether g is measured in money or in real terms), it should be pointed out that the value of the investment coefficient and thus the value of gk may depend to some extent on the behaviour of the general price level because of the way in which company accountants measure investment in stocks (see p. 111 above). Specifically, if stocks are valued on a 'first in, first out' basis, a rising general price level makes some investment in stocks necessary in each period merely to maintain a constant volume of stocks. In consequence, other things being equal, the faster the rate of inflation (which we shall regard as exogenously determined) the larger will be the investment coefficient. This would not be so if company accountants, like national income accountants, were to define investment in stocks as the increase in the volume of stocks valued at current prices; the size of gk would then be independent of the behaviour of the general price level.

One further transformation of variables is necessary in order to develop a model of the determination of the share of profits in national income ('national income' being a term which we shall illegitimately but harmlessly use interchangeably with 'gross national product'). In the previous chapter we defined the profit margin of the individual firm as the ratio of profits to sales revenue. The share of profits in national income, however, is the ratio of profits to value added (i.e. sales revenue plus changes in stocks minus purchases of intermediate inputs). It is therefore appropriate to redefine V as value added, π as the ratio of profits to value added, g as the proportional growth rate of value added and k as the ratio of investment to the absolute increase in value added. In each case, 'value added' (which in this connection should be interpreted as being gross of depreciation) is substituted for 'sales revenue' in the original definition. Although this substitution changes the numerical values of the variables involved, the accounting relationships which link them remain valid. More importantly, this substitution is insignificant as far as causation and behaviour are concerned, provided that we assume that in the long run the ratio of value added to sales revenue is determined independently of the other variables of the model.*

* In other words, we must assume that both the target ratio of stocks to sales and the ratio of intermediate inputs to value added are for all practical purposes exogenously determined.

Of the two fundamental relationships of our microeconomic model, one, the finance frontier

$$\pi \geqslant \frac{(1+f-x)}{r}gk$$

makes perfectly good sense when interpreted in macroeconomic terms. That is, we can say straightforwardly that the profit margin of the company sector must be at least great enough to provide finance for the company sector's investment. By contrast, the opportunity frontier $\pi \leqslant \mu(g, k)$ is specifically microeconomic in character. In particular, it was constructed on the 'partial equilibrium' assumption that the demand for the products of the individual firm depends only to a negligible extent on its own output level and investment outlays. This cannot plausibly be assumed to be the case for the company sector as a whole; the aggregate demand for the products of all firms taken together is likely to depend to a great extent on their aggregate output and aggregate investment outlays. For this reason, in constructing a model of the economy as a whole, we must abandon the opportunity frontier and replace it by some other, macroeconomic, relationship. Indeed, much of the present chapter will be devoted to precisely this exercise.

In the context of the company sector as a whole the opportunity frontiers of individual firms serve primarily to determine their growth rates relative to one another – and thus, at any moment of time, their relative sizes. For, since aggregate demand is always in some sense limited, expansion by each individual firm can occur only at the expense of the actual and potential sales of other firms. It is this, together with the urge to grow as fast as possible, which causes firms to compete against one another by innovation, advertising, price policy and other means. Thus the form of the individual firm's opportunity frontier, although it depends to some extent on the rate of growth of aggregate demand, is determined mainly by the effectiveness of the firm's production and selling policies in relation to those of other firms – or, in a word, by its competitiveness. At any particular time, firms vary widely in their competitiveness; over time, therefore, some grow much faster than others. Most grow in absolute size, but some shrink and a few go out of business altogether. The pattern of change does not remain the same; new management can revive flagging companies and successful ones can become complacent.

The details of this competitive struggle and of the pattern which emerges from it are of little relevance from a macroeconomic viewpoint. But the fact that a competitive struggle is occurring is, of fundamental importance to our macroeconomic model, because this struggle drives firms to their finance frontiers. For, as was explained in the previous chapter, no individual growth-maximising firm will choose a profit margin higher than the minimum financially necessary, since its expansion is also constrained by the demand for its products, which could be increased at the expense of other firms by reduction of its profit margin. As a result, the actual profit margin of the company sector will be equal in equilibrium to the minimum financially necessary profit margin.

For this reason, in developing our macroeconomic model, we shall introduce the finance frontier of the company sector, not in the form of an inequality, but as an equation, namely

$$\pi = \frac{(1+f-x)}{r} gk,$$

which states that the company sector profit margin is uniquely determined by the need to finance company sector investment. This relationship, which we shall rename the finance *function*, is the most important element of our macroeconomic model. In effect, it subsumes all three elements of our microeconomic model. In particular, the drive to maximise growth and the opportunity frontier, although they play no overt role, are in fact crucial to the macroeconomic model, since they press the company sector profit margin down to a specific level determined by finance requirements, thus enabling us to transform the finance frontier from an inequality into an equation.

In other words, it is competition, a microeconomic phenomenon, which renders our macroeconomic model determinate and sets a limit on the share of profits in national income – and once again it must be stressed that we refer to all forms of competition and not solely to price competition. In order that competition should have this effect, it is not, of course, necessary to suppose that any particular firm is, or regards itself as, in direct competition at any moment with more than a limited range of other firms. Companies alter their product mixes and patterns of rivalries over time, being guided by what they regard as the most effective strategies for growth. Nor is it necessary to suppose that company sales strategies always involve uninhibited competition with all rivals. Firms may find it expedient to make alliances with certain other firms in particular product lines in order to devote more of their efforts to competition with other firms in other product lines.

What is essential, though, is that the company sector should contain many firms and that each of these firms should be striving to grow at the expense of at least some of its rivals. For if the company sector actually or effectively consisted of a single huge firm, and there were no foreign competition, the present model would become indeterminate, since there would be no reason for the finance frontier to bind. But the capitalist economies to which the model relates, although they exhibit a lack of competition in certain markets, are very far from being monopolistic in this ultimate sense; in general, indeed, the individualistic, expansionist, competitive spirit of capitalism remains very much in evidence. (Incidentally, in this context one cannot talk in any meaningful way about the 'degree of monopoly' of the company sector as a whole. The company sector either is or is not competitive in the present sense; the distinction involved is one of kind not degree.)*

The conclusions of this section may be summarised as follows. The company sector profit margin is governed by the need to finance company sector investment, the extent of which depends on the company sector growth rate and the company sector investment coefficient. The size of the necessary profit margin depends on company sector financial behaviour, which is reflected in the values taken on by the financial asset ratio, the external finance ratio and the gross retention ratio, which we shall regard as exogenously determined by the considerations discussed in chapters 2 and 3.

* This is the reason why it was asserted at the beginning of chapter 1 that the present theory of the determination of the share of profits is not a 'degree of monopoly' theory of the type developed by Kalecki (e.g. 1952, chs. 1 and 2). One can, of course, always make meaningful statements about the degree of monopoly of individual firms or markets. Indeed, the differing degrees of monopoly of particular firms with respect to particular products exercise an important influence on the forms of their opportunity frontiers and thus on their relative growth rates and profit margins.

This financial relationship, which is formally expressed in the finance function, constitutes the core of our theory of the share of profits. But to complete the theory it is evidently necessary to explain what determines the rate of growth of company sector output and the value of the company sector investment coefficient, and to investigate the relationship between the company sector profit margin and the share of profits in national income. These tasks will occupy us for much of the present chapter. As in the previous chapter, most of the argument will relate exclusively to the long run, although we shall comment briefly on the behaviour of the share of profits in the short run. In addition, in the course of developing the theory, we shall discuss a number of related matters, such as the incidence of taxes on profits, and we shall make some comparisons between the present theory and other theories of the share of profits.

4.2 A BASIC MODEL

We shall start by setting out a simple version of our model of the determination of the share of profits in the long run. Its simplicity is the result of a number of restrictive assumptions, all of which will subsequently be relaxed. In particular, we shall assume for the time being (1) that the economy is closed, (2) that there is no government (although there is money), (3) that all output is produced by the company sector (although there is a passive system of financial intermediaries), (4) that the output of the economy is not constrained by the availability of labour, (5) that the company sector investment coefficient may be regarded as an exogenously determined variable and (6) that long run equilibrium prevails in the sense that stocks, the degree of capacity use, short term borrowing, financial asset holdings and the payout ratio are at their long run target levels.

An immediate advantage of these assumptions is that they simplify the relationship between the share of profits in national income and the company sector profit margin. For, since the economy is closed and all output is produced by the company sector, national income and company sector output are one and the same thing, and thus the share of profits in national income is identically equal to the company sector profit margin.

Furthermore, the last assumption ensures that the company sector profit margin is at the target level specified by the finance function.

Another advantage of these assumptions is that they enable us to give a relatively simple account of the determination of the rate of growth of company sector output (i.e. of national income). To begin with, because capacity is always at least equal to demand in long run equilibrium, and because there is no shortage of labour, the level of output must be determined by the level of effective demand. In the Keynesian manner, we shall suppose demand to be made up of two components.

(a) Autonomous demand, being expenditure which is independent of the current level of output or income. This consists of company sector investment plus another item, which we shall label A and which we shall interpret provisionally as that part of consumption expenditure which is unaffected by the current level of household income.

(b) Induced demand, being expenditure which is directly dependent on the current level of output or income. Let the (average and marginal) propensity to spend out of income generated in the company sector be $(1-l)$, l being the proportional leakage of income into, for example, savings. For simplicity let us assume *provisionally* that l is strictly exogenously determined and in particular that its size does not depend on the share of profits in company sector output.

In consequence, ignoring all lags, the equilibrium level of output, V, is determined by the relationship

$$V = \frac{I+A}{l} \tag{1}$$

which is the multiplier equation. Given the level of output in the preceding period, the multiplier also determines the growth of output in the current period.

Let us now ask what governs the level of investment. It follows directly from the model of behaviour developed in the last chapter that the amount of investment which firms will undertake in any given long period is determined by how much additional capacity they expect to need, in conjunction with their chosen investment coefficients (which determine the amounts of investment required to provide a unit increase in capacity). In equilibrium, since expectations are fulfilled, the initial level of excess capacity will be zero and the actual growth of demand (and thus of output) will be equal to the expected growth of demand. This being so, the level of investment is determined by the relationship

$$I = k.gV, \tag{2}$$

which is a version of the accelerator principle.

Thus the rate of growth of output both influences and is influenced by the level of investment. In order for the degree of capacity use to be maintained at its target level, which is one of the conditions of equilibrium, these two channels of influence must be consistent with one another in the sense that the level of investment must be such as to cause the growth of demand over the period to be equal to the growth of capacity. This 'balancing' level of investment s associated with a particul ar rate of growth, which we shall call the equilibrium rate of growth. In formal terms the equilibrium growth rate must satisfy both the multiplier relationship and the accelerator relationship. In consequence, by substituting the accelerator relationship into the multiplier relationship and rearranging, one can derive an equation which specifies the equilibrium value of the growth rate.* It is

$$g = \frac{l-a}{k-a} \tag{3}$$

where
$$a = \frac{A}{\tilde{V}}$$

being the ratio of current autonomous demand (other than company sector investment) to output in the previous period. (The reason for introducing autonomous demand in this particular manner is that $A/\tilde{V}$ is a ratio which is strictly independent of the other variables of the model in a way that, for example, the ratio A/V is not.)

The equation which determines the equilibrium growth rate, which we may suppose to refer either to a single long period or to a situation of steady state growth, is a generalisation of Harrod's expression for the warranted growth rate. It is a generalisation

* Specifically, one substitutes kgV for I and $\tilde{V}/(1-g)$ for V (since $g \equiv (V-\tilde{V})/V$) in the multiplier equation $V = (I+A)/l$ and rearranges.

inasmuch as it introduces sources of autonomous demand other than investment (and, as we shall see, it can accommodate *all* types of autonomous expenditures and leakages). If company sector investment were the only source of autonomous demand (i.e. if the variable a were set equal to zero), the equation would reduce to Harrod's original expression, namely

$$g = \frac{l}{k} \qquad (4)$$

which is a special case about which more will be said below. The properties of the present equation are fairly straightforward, at any rate over the range of practical interest.* Other things being equal, the equilibrium growth rate increases as the size of the proportional leakage increases, and decreases as the size of the investment coefficient increases. The equilibrium growth rate also decreases as the level of autonomous consumption expenditure increases. This makes economic sense; given the size of the proportional leakage, which determines the ratio of investment plus autonomous consumption to national income,† a higher level of autonomous consumption must imply a lower ratio of investment to national income, which, given any particular value of the investment coefficient (the incremental capital–output ratio), must cause a lower rate of growth of capacity and thus of output.

We are now in a position to assemble a complete model of the determination of the share of profits, by combining this account of the determination of the growth rate with the description of financial behaviour summarised in the finance function. Formally, substituting the equation which determines the equilibrium growth rate into the finance function, we obtain

$$\pi = \frac{(1+f-x)}{r} \left(\frac{l-a}{k-a}\right) k. \qquad (5)$$

* Which is $a < l < k$. If no restrictions are placed on the values of the variables involved, the equation behaves badly in various respects.
† This, by the way, is not the same thing as saying that the absolute level oɪ investment is determined by the absolute level of savings. For, as we have seen, the absolute level of investment in this simple model is determined by the accelerator, and the operation of the multiplier causes the level of income to be such as to bring the absolute level of savings into line with the absolute level of investment. The size of the proportional leakage governs only the *ratio* of investment to national income.

The substance of this equation is that, given the values of the three financial ratios, the share of profits is determined by the need to generate the right amount of cash to finance company sector investment, the extent of which depends on the rate of growth of output, which in turn depends on the interaction of the multiplier and the accelerator. Other things being equal, the higher the equilibrium growth rate, and thus the higher the ratio of investment to national income, the greater will be the share of profits. Similarly, the share of profits will be greater, the lower are the external finance ratio and the gross retention ratio and the higher is the financial asset ratio, all of which tend to increase the amount of profits needed to finance any particular amount of investment.

The share of profits evidently also depends on the value of the investment coefficient, which we are provisionally treating as an exogenously determined variable. It is clear from equation (5) that the investment coefficient has two different sorts of influence on the share of profits, since it enters into both the finance function and the equation which determines the equilibrium growth rate. Moreover, these two influences act in opposite directions. For example, an increase in the investment coefficient, although it tends to increase the share of profits by raising the finance requirements associated with any particular growth rate, also tends to reduce the share of profits by reducing the equilibrium rate of growth, since a given ratio of investment to national income now generates a smaller proportional increase in capacity. In general, the latter tendency is stronger than the former; that is, the net effect of an increase in the investment coefficient would be to reduce the share of profits.* But in a special case, the two tendencies are of equal size and thus cancel one another out.

The special case in question is that in which company sector investment is the only source of autonomous demand (i.e. in which a is equal to zero). For this causes the investment coefficient to disappear from equation (5), which becomes

$$\pi = \frac{(1+f-x)}{r}l. \tag{6}$$

* This can be seen by reducing equation (5) to

$$\pi = \frac{(1+f-x)}{r}\left(\frac{l-a}{1-a/k}\right)$$

in which k appears only once. Given that $a < l < k$, it follows that $\partial\pi/\partial k < 0$.

This result, although it arises only under restrictive assumptions, is of interest because it suggests that in certain circumstances the share of profits might be unaffected by a whole complex of considerations to which great importance is conventionally attached, namely the nature of technology, the criteria for choosing particular techniques and so on. But in general the share of profits does depend on the investment coefficient. For this reason, in order to complete the model, it is essential to give a fuller account of the way in which the value of the aggregate investment coefficient is determined. This will be undertaken in the next section.

At this point, however, let us investigate the consequences of relaxing the assumption that the size of the proportional leakage, l, is independent of the size of the share of profits (which is both unrealistic and inconsistent with one of the central tenets of the neo-Keynesian theory of distribution). The most general way to do this is to write l as $l(\pi)$, leaving open for the moment the form of the relationship between l and π. This modification makes the present model a little more complicated, but does not alter its essential character. In particular, it remains the case that the share of profits is determined by the finance function in conjunction with the equilibrium growth rate. However, the equilibrium growth rate itself now depends in part on the size of the share of profits.

This can be demonstrated formally by rewriting equation (3) which determines the equilibrium growth rate. It becomes

$$g = \frac{l(\pi) - a}{k - a}. \tag{7}$$

In consequence, equation (5) which determines the share of profits becomes

$$\pi = \frac{(1 + f - x)}{r} \left(\frac{l(\pi) - a}{k - a} \right) k, \tag{8}$$

which can be solved for π (and in most cases rearranged in such a way that π appears only on the left-hand side) provided that we specify the form of the relationship between l and π.* In this

---

* The resulting value of π can then be used to solve equation (7). Incidentally, since l is in general an increasing function of π, the 'qualitative' properties of the model are unaltered by this modification. For example, it remains true that an increase in a will reduce π, that an increase in f will increase π, etc.

regard there are various possibilities, of which two are of particular interest.

(1) The neo-Keynesian theorists of distribution originally postulated that the relationship between l and π was of the form

$$l = s_p\pi + s_w(1-\pi), \tag{9}$$

where s_p is the propensity to save out of profits and s_w is the propensity to save out of other sorts of income. Substituting this expression into equation (8) above (and assuming for convenience that a is zero) we can derive a new equation which determines the share of profits, namely

$$\pi = \frac{s_w}{r/(1+f-x)-s_p+s_w}. \tag{10}$$

It is important to note that this last equation, though to some extent of neo-Keynesian form, is bereft of neo-Keynesian substance (see also the discussion and footnotes on pp. 13–15, 124–5 and 133). This can be illustrated in a formal way by comparing it with the basic equation of the neo-Keynesian theory of distribution, which is

$$\pi = \frac{1}{(s_p-s_w)}\textsl{g}k - \frac{s_w}{(s_p-s_w)}, \tag{11}$$

where $\textsl{g}$ must be interpreted as some exogenously determined growth rate (such as the natural rate of growth). Apart from anything else, the two equations (10 and 11) contain different (but overlapping) sets of variables. In addition, the two equations exhibit different properties with respect to those variables which they have in common. For example, equation (10) would collapse if s_w were set equal to zero, a contingency which would leave the neo-Keynesian equation unscathed. Conversely, the neo-Keynesian equation would collapse if s_p were equal to s_w, a contingency which would leave equation (10) unscathed.

(2) Alternatively, one could regard total savings as the sum of retained profits and savings out of household income (dividends, interest and income from employment). The relationship between l and π would therefore be

$$l = r\pi + s(1-r\pi), \tag{12}$$

where s is the propensity to save out of household income, which we shall assume for simplicity to be independent both of the composition of household income and of the extent of capital gains on ordinary shares caused by the retention of profits.*† If we substitute this expression into equation (8) above (continuing to assume that a is zero) we can derive yet another equation which determines the share of profits, namely

$$\pi = \frac{s}{r\{1/(1+f-x)-(1-s)\}}. \qquad (13)$$

So far we have considered only one specific type of leakage, namely saving. This is appropriate in the context of a closed economy with no government. But in subsequent sections it will

* Incidentally, given a closed economy with no government, the sum of household savings (i.e. the household sector's net acquisition of financial assets) and the company sector's net acquisition of financial assets must be zero. In equilibrium, therefore

$$s(1-r\pi)V+(f-x)I = 0.$$

This can be rewritten as

$$s(1-r\pi)V+fI = xI.$$

The left-hand side of this equation could be interpreted as the demand function for new issues of company sector securities and the right-hand side as the supply function of new issues of company sector securities.

† Except in one special case both these assumptions could be relaxed without altering the substance of the model. The special case in question would arise in the context of Kaldor's Neo-Pasinetti Theorem (see Kaldor, 1966, and Davidson, 1968), the essence of which is that the aggregate valuation ratio (i.e. the relationship between retained profits and capital gains) is assumed to be a passive, endogenously determined, variable. As a result, s (i.e. the household sector's net acquisition of financial assets as a ratio of household income from dividends, interest and employment), which in Kaldor's model depends on the extent of capital gains, also becomes an endogenously determined variable. In consequence, the equilibrium growth rate becomes indeterminate; induced changes in the aggregate valuation ratio will bring demand into line with capacity, no matter what the rate of growth of capacity. Kaldor eliminates this indeterminacy from his model by requiring that the equilibrium growth rate be equal to some exogenously determined growth rate (such as the natural rate of growth). It would be possible to develop the present model along similar lines. However, I do not believe that the aggregate valuation ratio is in fact determined in the manner postulated by Kaldor. In particular, since in reality the interest rate is determined by governmental monetary policy and share prices also depend heavily on volatile and speculative expectations of the future, I believe it to be more appropriate to treat the aggregate valuation ratio as an exogenously determined variable; see also p. 133n below.

be necessary to introduce other types of leakages, the most important being taxation and imports. This will make the form of the relationship between l and π much more complicated. But these additional complications do not affect the substance of the present theory in any fundamental way. In most of what follows, therefore, we shall simplify the exposition by assuming once again that the size of the proportional leakage, l, is strictly independent of the size of the share of profits.

4.3 THE INVESTMENT COEFFICIENT

In this section we shall consider the determination of the aggregate investment coefficient in greater detail. It is convenient to begin by recalling the principles according to which the investment coefficient is determined at the level of the individual firm (these are set out more fully on pp. 86–90). Two opposing forces are involved: (1) the favourable effect of a higher investment coefficient on the demand–profit margin tradeoff, which would tend to increase the firm's growth rate; (2) the adverse effect of a higher investment coefficient on the finance frontier, which would tend to decrease the firm's growth rate. The firm chooses that particular value of the investment coefficient at which these two forces balance in the sense that the maximum possible rate of growth is attained. This approach is fairly similar to that which would be adopted by an orthodox cost-minimising firm (although the implicit target yield on investment is determined in an unorthodox way).* The similarity is valuable because it enables us to draw on a number of established propositions relating to the determination of the investment coefficient.

Given these general principles, the precise value of the investment coefficient chosen by the firm depends on the form of the finance frontier (and in particular on the values of the financial asset ratio, the external finance ratio and the gross retention ratio) and on the form of the opportunity frontier. The latter depends

---

* See the discussion of yield calculations on pp. 97–100 above. Another, less important, difference arises from the fact that in the present model the firm is endeavouring to maximise its sales revenue rather than its profits; this affects the investment coefficient because in general a sales-maximising firm will differ from a profit-maximising firm with regard to its price levels and the commodity composition of its output.

on such things as (a) the conditions of demand for the various commodities which the firm might produce, (b) the nature of the techniques available for producing and selling these commodities, (c) the prices of inputs, including labour and capital goods, (d) managerial attitudes towards risk and (e) the history of the firm – its inheritance of product lines and equipment.*

This account of the determination of the investment coefficient at the level of the individual firm also constitutes the basis of our explanation of the value of the aggregate investment coefficient, which is simply a weighted average of the investment coefficients of all the individual firms of which the company sector is composed. In the previous section, in order to simplify the argument, we treated the aggregate investment coefficient as if it were an exogenously determined variable. In the remainder of the present section, we shall investigate the ways in which the value of the investment coefficient might be dependent on the other variables of our macroeconomic model, particularly the company sector profit margin, the growth rate and the three financial ratios. For, in so far as the aggregate investment coefficient is an endogenously determined variable, the pattern of causation in our macroeconomic model must be more complex than has so far been suggested.

In the context of our partial equilibrium model of the individual firm, we can derive certain specific propositions about the way in which the value of the investment coefficient depends on the several variables which, in their aggregate forms, appear in our macroeconomic model. In particular, it is probable that there is some tendency for a lower investment coefficient to be chosen, (a) the higher the growth rate, (b) the higher the financial asset ratio, (c) the lower the external finance ratio and (d) the lower the gross retention ratio. To see why this is so, it is appropriate to refer back to our earlier discussion of yield calculations (pp. 97–100). As a general rule, for very orthodox reasons, the number of investment projects which the firm will regard as sufficiently attractive to undertake will be smaller, the higher the target yield with which their individual rates of return must be compared. For example,

* The form of the opportunity frontier and thus the chosen value of the investment coefficient may also depend to some extent on the rate of change of prices; see, for example, p. 67n above.

a target yield of 10 per cent might make it worthwhile to replace machines of both 1955 and 1965 vintages, while a target yield of 20 per cent might cause the firm to regard as attractive only the replacement of the 1955 vintage. Other things being equal, then, it is reasonable to suppose that in practice a higher target yield will tend to cause the firm to choose a lower investment co-efficient.*

In the present model, the size of the target yield, $\hat{\rho}$, is determined by a relationship of the form

$$\hat{\rho} = \frac{(1+f-x)}{r}(g_K + \delta)$$

which is a modified version of the finance frontier. It is clear from this expression that (a) the higher the growth rate, (b) the higher the financial asset ratio, (c) the lower the external finance ratio and (d) the lower the gross retention ratio, the higher will be the target yield and thus (as was asserted at the outset) the lower will be the investment coefficient chosen by the firm. The economic meaning of this is as follows. The higher are the growth rate and the financial asset ratio, and the lower are the external finance ratio and the gross retention ratio, the greater is the amount of profits that will be required to provide finance for capacity expansion at any given value of the investment coefficient. In consequence, the need to keep down the size of the investment coefficient becomes more pressing. That is, the higher the rate of profit that the firm must on average earn in order to finance its investment, the more reluctant will it be to divert funds into investment projects with relatively low yields.

At the level of the individual firm, then, one can arrive at certain relatively straightforward conclusions about the behaviour of the investment coefficient in relation to the other variables of the model. This is unfortunately not the case at an aggregate level, because, broadly speaking, it is no longer legitimate to treat relative prices and quantities as exogenously given. Let us consider, for example, three additional sorts of effect which an autonomous

* There may be some exceptions to this rule. In principle it is possible that the character of the alternatives available might be such that a higher target yield would cause the firm to choose a higher investment coefficient.

increase in the aggregate growth rate might have on the value of the aggregate investment coefficient.

(a) Let us suppose to begin with that the growth rates of all commodities increase by the same proportion. Given the general form of the finance frontier, this will tend to cause the profit margins on all commodities to increase by an equal proportion. This in turn will cause relative price changes; in particular, there will be a rise in the prices of goods on which profit margins are high in relation to the prices of goods on which profit margins are low.* Thus, among other things, there will be a rise in the prices of goods which are produced by capital-intensive methods (i.e. in industries in which investment coefficients are high) relative to the prices of goods produced by less capital-intensive methods. And if, as seems likely in practice, investment goods are produced by more capital-intensive methods than other goods, this relative price change will cause the aggregate investment coefficient to rise.† Thus, in opposition to the tendency discerned at the level of the individual firm, there will be a tendency for a higher growth rate to be associated with a higher investment coefficient.

(b) This will be compounded by the fact that, other things being equal, a higher aggregate growth rate necessarily entails a higher ratio of investment to national income. For, since investment goods are produced by more capital-intensive methods than other goods, investment coefficients in capital goods industries are higher than in other industries. Thus an increase in the share (or weight) of the capital goods industries in total output will raise the aggregate investment coefficient, which is a weighted average of the investment coefficients in all the individual industries of which the economy is composed.

* Consider, for example, two goods, A and B, each of which has unit costs of £1. Let the initial profit margins on A and B be 40 per cent and 20 per cent respectively, and let both profit margins increase by a factor of one half, to 60 per cent and 30 per cent respectively. Applying the formula $p = c/(1-\pi)$, where p = price and c = unit cost, it will be observed that this causes the price ratio p_A/p_B to increase (from about 1.33 to about 1.75); that is, the price of the good with the higher profit margin increases relative to the price of the good with the lower profit margin.
† This being a 'negative price Wicksell effect' (see Harcourt, 1972, pp. 39–45). In principle, of course, the price Wicksell effect might be positive; this would tend to cause a higher aggregate growth rate to be associated with a lower investment coefficient.

(c) Against this, however, it should be noted that, other things being equal, the increase in the share of profits caused by the higher aggregate growth rate will cause a fall in the real wage rate; that is, it will raise the prices of investment goods (and indeed of all commodities) in relation to the money wage rate. This will tend to cause the choice of a lower investment coefficient because it makes the substitution of capital for labour a less attractive proposition. Thus, for example, a fall in the real wage rate will tend to cause fewer replacement projects to be undertaken.

Examples of this kind could be multiplied, bringing in other variables and other relationships. But two things are already plain. (1) It is not strictly legitimate to assume that the value of the aggregate investment coefficient is exogenously given. In other words, the descriptive accuracy of our macroeconomic model would be increased if, instead of treating the investment coefficient as an independently determined variable, we were to include an additional equation specifying the effects which changes in the other variables of the model would have on the value of the aggregate investment coefficient. (2) But nothing simple can be said *a priori* about the character of this equation, since it involves several different influences, not all of which pull in the same direction and about whose relative magnitudes it is impossible to generalise.* For instance, of the four effects of an increase in the growth rate considered above, two tend to raise the investment coefficient and two tend to lower it, and there is no reason to suppose that in general the former tendency would outweigh the latter, or vice versa.

However, as a first approximation to reality, we shall probably not be too greatly in error if we ignore this pattern of interdependence altogether. For in practice the quantitative importance of these 'endogenous' influences on the value of the investment coefficient is likely to be small, both in relation to other, exogenous, influences on the investment coefficient (such as the nature of available technology) and in relation to the other influences on the magnitude of the share of profits with which the present model deals. From this point onwards, therefore, we shall

* This being to a considerable extent the upshot of the recent controversies in capital theory; see Harcourt (1972).

for the most part proceed as if the aggregate investment coefficient were an exogenously determined variable, in effect reverting to our original simplifying assumption.

4.4 THE SUPPLY OF LABOUR AND THE REAL WAGE

In setting out a simple model of the determination of the share of profits in the second section of this chapter, we assumed that the output of the economy was not constrained by the availability of labour, meaning by this that the number of men seeking jobs was not less than the number of jobs offered. In this section we shall examine the implications of this assumption more closely. We shall continue to assume that we are dealing with a closed economy without a government in which all output is produced by the company sector and which is in a state of equilibrium in the sense that the expectations of businessmen are fulfilled.

Let us suppose to begin with that, even though full capacity use (and thus full employment in the Keynesian sense) prevails by assumption, the number of men seeking jobs exceeds the number of jobs available, or, in other words, that there is a certain amount of Marxian unemployment. From the point of view of the present theory, what is significant about unemployment of this sort is that it need show no tendency to disappear. That is to say, the model set out earlier contains no mechanism which would tend automatically to eliminate excess supply in the labour market; indeed, the presence of a reserve army is perfectly consistent with the existence of equilibrium in the sense in which we are using the term. Nor, it should be stressed, is this in any way dependent on the real wage being unable to fall below some subsistence minimum.

In this regard, the present theory diverges from, and would appear to be more realistic than, most neo-Keynesian and neo-classical theories of economic growth, which postulate (in their weak forms) that the presence of Marxian unemployment is inconsistent with equilibrium and (in their strong forms) that there are forces in the economy which tend to eliminate Marxian unemployment. It is therefore of some interest to examine these neo-Keynesian and neoclassical theories and to point out the respects in which they differ from the present theory. In order to abbreviate and simplify this investigation, we shall confine it to the familiar framework of steady growth models.* In this context, the present theory, by contrast with the neo-Keynesian and neo-classical theories, implies that there is no reason why, in equilibrium, the natural rate of growth should not exceed the warranted rate.

In the standard type of neo-Keynesian model, Marxian unemployment can be eliminated by an increase in the share of profits, which raises the economy's propensity to save and thus, given the value of the investment coefficient, increases the warranted growth rate. In other words, there is a particular value of the share of profits which would cause the warranted growth rate to equal the natural growth rate, and in this type of neo-Keynesian model equilibrium is attained only when the share of profits takes on that value. In the present model, however, even if we make the propensity to save a function of the share of profits, there is in effect one less degree of freedom; the share of profits is determined by the need to finance the warranted growth rate of the capital stock, and therefore it is not free to adjust to the level necessary to eliminate Marxian unemployment. Indeed, we have already formally demonstrated this to be the case by showing that, under identical assumptions about the influence of the share of profits on the propensity to save, the basic equation of the neo-Keynesian model and the basic equation of the present model yield different values for the share of profits.†

The neoclassical mechanism for the elimination of Marxian unemployment is rather different (although it is not inconsistent with the neo-Keynesian mechanism – cf. Hahn and Matthews, 1965, section I.5(b)). To consider it, we must relax our assumption that the value of the investment coefficient is exogenously

* With particular reference to Hahn and Matthews (1965).

† P. 117 above, interpreting g as the natural rate of growth. Not all neo-Keynesian economists would interpret g as the natural rate or would argue that Marxian unemployment tends to be eliminated. Joan Robinson in particular regards g as being independently determined by animal spirits. In her model, then, which differs both from the present theory and from what I am calling the standard type of neo-Keynesian theory, there is no reason why there should not be a reserve army of labour. Moreover, the present theory does not logically preclude the possibility that Kaldor's Neo-Pasinetti mechanism (see p. 118n above) might bring the warranted rate of growth into line with the natural rate. But see n * on p. 133 below.

determined. The basic principle of the neoclassical mechanism is that excess supply in the labour market will cause a fall in the real wage, which will induce firms to adopt more labour-intensive techniques of production, thus increasing the amount of employment available. In particular, it will cause the choice of a lower value of the aggregate investment coefficient which, given the size of the propensity to save, will increase the warranted growth rate.

The smooth working of this mechanism may be obstructed in various familiar ways; not least, the aggregate production function may be 'badly behaved' or the real wage may encounter a lower bound at or above zero. But for the purpose of comparing the neoclassical theory with the present theory, it is convenient to assume these potential obstructions away. For the point of the comparison is quite different; it is that in the present theory there is one less degree of freedom than in the neoclassical theory. In the present theory, the real wage is determined by the need for profits to be such as to finance the warranted growth rate, and thus, even with the best-behaved type of production function, it is not free to adjust to the level which would eliminate Marxian unemployment.

One way of demonstrating this formally is by converting the present model of the determination of the share of profits into an account of the determination of the aggregate profit rate, ρ. In a steady state context, neglecting depreciation and autonomous expenditure other than company sector investment, we obtain an equation of the form

$$\rho = \frac{(1+f-x)}{r}\frac{l}{k}$$

which states that the profit rate depends on the warranted growth rate via the three financial ratios.* If this equation were introduced

* The equation is derived by modifying the finance function (p. 109) in the same sort of way that the finance frontier was modified on p. 98 above. One first multiplies the finance function through by $V/\overline{K}$, the inverse of the average capital-output ratio (bearing in mind the definitions of π, g and k on p. 69). Since $P/\overline{K} \equiv \rho$ and $I/\overline{K} \equiv g_K+\delta+\lambda$, the resulting expression can be rewritten as $\rho = (1+f-x)(g_K+\delta+\lambda)/r$. One then sets δ and λ equal to zero (for simplicity), $g_K = g$ (by virtue of the assumption of steady state), and $g = l/k$ (this being the equation which determines the equilibrium growth rate in the special case in which $a = 0$).

into a standard neoclassical growth model, it would cause over-determinacy; there would be more equations than unknown variables.* This overdeterminacy could be avoided by dropping the neoclassical requirement that the warranted growth rate be equal to the natural growth rate, thus permitting the presence of Marxian unemployment in equilibrium.

It remains to enquire what would happen if, by contrast with what we have so far assumed to be the case, the output of the economy were to be constrained by the availability of labour in the sense that the number of men seeking jobs was less than the number of jobs offered. For, from the point of view of the present theory, although excess supply in the labour market is perfectly consistent with the existence of equilibrium, excess demand in the labour market is not, since it causes underutilisation of capacity (simply because some capacity cannot be manned). Thus, unlike a surplus of labour, a shortage of labour must have some impact in the context of the present model (especially since we have shown that the demand for labour cannot be brought into line with the supply by the neo-Keynesian or the neoclassical mechanisms).

In a situation of labour scarcity of this sort, one possible way out, which will be discussed in subsequent sections, would be to abandon one or more of our simplifying assumptions (such as the assumption that equilibrium prevails). However, there are two other mechanisms whereby excess demand in the labour market can be reduced in a way which is consistent with the simple version of the model set out in the second section of this chapter. Both mechanisms are of considerable importance in reality.

(1) A shortage of labour stimulates technical progress in the form of labour-saving inventions of various kinds. (Conversely, an induced fall in the rate of technical progress might reduce Marxian unemployment. But this can occur only to a limited extent, since there is no such thing as negative technical progress. Indeed, the

---

* The same would be true if the equation were introduced into the sort of combined neo-Keynesian–neoclassical model which is discussed by Hahn and Matthews (1965) in section I.5(b) of their survey. Strictly speaking, we ought also to take account of the fact that, at any particular rate of profit, the technique of production chosen by the profit maximising firms of neoclassical theory would not be exactly the same as that chosen by the growth maximising firms of the present theory (see p. 119n above). However, the differences are of a kind which is not crucial in this particular connection.

competitive struggle between firms would cause the rate of technical progress to be positive even in the face of a large reserve army of
labour.)

(2) A shortage of labour causes firms to adopt more capital-
intensive techniques of production than would otherwise have been
appropriate at the prevailing level of the real wage. This occurs
because the supply of labour to individual firms becomes less
elastic with respect to changes in wages and recruitment expenditures, thus widening the gap between the prevailing wage rate and
the marginal cost of obtaining additional labour (for it is the latter,
not the former, which is relevant to the choice of technique).*
The resultant increase in the aggregate investment coefficient
reduces the equilibrium rate of growth and hence the demand for
labour. (Conversely, an induced increase in the elasticity of the
supply of labour to individual firms could help to absorb Marxian
unemployment. But again there is an asymmetry, because the
supply of labour can never be more than infinitely elastic. That is,
the marginal cost of additional labour can never be less than the
prevailing wage rate.)

4.5 DISEQUILIBRIUM AND DEMAND MANAGEMENT

Up to this point in the present chapter, we have proceeded as if the
economy were in equilibrium in two interrelated respects. First,
we have assumed that short term borrowing, financial asset holdings and the payout ratio are at their long run target levels and
thus that the company sector profit margin is determined in the
manner described by the finance function. Secondly, and more
fundamentally, we have assumed that stocks and the degree of
capacity use are at their long run target levels and thus that the
actual growth rate of company sector output is equal to the
equilibrium growth rate.

The purpose of this section is to discuss in particular the second
of these assumptions, which appears to be incompatible with the
views of both Keynes, who believed that capitalist economies do

---

* This suggestion is due to Kaldor; see Hahn and Matthews (1965) p. 19.
  This mechanism differs from the neoclassical mechanism described above, in
  which the elasticity of the supply of labour to individual firms is treated as
  exogenously given – it is normally assumed to be infinite.

not tend towards full capacity use, and Harrod, who argued that capitalist economies tend to move away from full capacity use.* For, although individual firms are continually making adjustments towards equilibrium, we have as yet given no reason why firms in aggregate should behave in such a way as to generate a rate of growth of demand which is consistent with their expectations of the rate of growth of demand. It is convenient to treat this subject in four stages.

(1) The present model deals with the determination of the share of profits in the long run. In consequence, the term 'equilibrium' must always be interpreted as meaning 'long run equilibrium'. For, as was explained in the previous chapter, long run equilibrium is entirely consistent with the existence of what we called short run disequilibrium. Specifically, although in any given year stocks, capacity use, short term borrowing, financial asset holdings and the payout ratio are in practice likely to deviate to a significant extent from their target levels, not all of these deviations will be regarded by firms as symptomatic of long run disequilibrium. Indeed, even though they cannot predict their extent and timing with accuracy, firms are bound to expect temporary discrepancies to occur for a wide variety of reasons.

Short run disequilibrium as such causes no alteration of target profit margins or of other aspects of companies' long run policies. But year to year fluctuations in the degree of capacity use do cause short run fluctuations of the share of profits around its long run target level. For, to recapitulate the argument of the last chapter, the existence of overhead costs of various sorts means that variations in the level of output from a given amount of capacity are associated with proportionally smaller variations in costs and proportionally greater variations in profits. Thus short run increases and decreases in aggregate demand, by causing changes in the degree of capacity use, give rise to short run increases and decreases in the share of profits which must be superimposed on the picture given by our long run model of the determination of the share of profits at normal full capacity use.

(2) But the most important implication of the fact that firms take a long run view is that the economy is in reality much more

* See, for example, the discussion of Harrod's model in section 1.7 of Hahn and Matthews (1965).

stable than Harrod and others have suggested. For, since firms plan over a three to five year horizon, their expectations of demand growth are based on the extrapolation of secular trends and are very inelastic with respect to year to year changes in demand. Short run fluctuations in demand, except in so far as they alter firms' views of the secular trend, will simply be absorbed by fluctuations in stocks and the degree of capacity use, without causing corresponding fluctuations in capacity installation and investment plans.

This short run flexibility, and in particular the maintenance of long run policies in the face of year to year changes in demand, imparts a good deal of stability to the economy. This is true, first, of employment behaviour; the company sector wage bill (and thus expenditure out of wages) varies less in the short run than the value of company sector output, because firms tend to treat labour of all types as an overhead in the short run. It is true also of behaviour with respect to investment and dividends, which are as far as possible kept at their long run levels regardless of short run variations in profits, by means of fluctuations in the payout ratio, short term borrowing and financial asset holdings around their long run target levels. Thus a short run change of any given magnitude in the demand for company sector output will cause a proportionally smaller change in the level of expenditure of companies and of those whose incomes arise in the company sector.

This sort of behaviour makes it unlikely that a chance departure from equilibrium will lead to a cumulative tendency away from equilibrium. Indeed, the propensity of businessmen to think in terms of trends and to ignore temporary deviations from long run targets makes it likely that a multiplier-accelerator growth path, once established, would be of a rather stable character.* In this respect, the present model differs from that of Harrod, which was based on the assumption that the investment plans of firms are very sensitive to year to year changes in the level of

* For the concept of a 'normal' growth rate (like the concept of a 'normal' interest rate) is a self-justifying phenomenon. Departures from it tend to generate expectations, not of further movement in the same direction, but of movement in the opposite direction. This principle has been embodied in a formal model by Rose; see Hahn and Matthews (1965) section 1.7.

demand and the degree of capacity use. However, the insensitivity of firms to short run shocks does not in itself constitute an adequate reason for supposing that long run equilibrium is a normal state of affairs. For disequilibrium can be caused by many sorts of autonomous disturbances, not all of which are short run in nature, and there is nothing in the present model which would inevitably produce a general tendency towards equilibrium.

(3) But at this juncture it is appropriate to relax our assumption that there is no government (although we shall provisionally continue to assume that the economy is closed and that all output is produced by the company sector). For the modern capitalist economies to which the present theory relates are characterised by substantial government intervention in the area of demand management. The most important implement of demand management is fiscal policy (although credit control also plays a significant role in the short run). For even though, under the present assumptions, the government produces no output of its own, it can purchase company sector output and levy taxes. Government spending enters the model as a further source of autonomous demand and taxation exercises an influence through its effects on the propensity to spend out of income generated in the company sector.

In a modern economy, it is reasonable to assume that fiscal policy is used purposively and that the government manages the level of demand in accordance with certain specific policy objectives. One of these objectives, which, as we shall see in a later section (p. 146 below), is unlikely to conflict with the government's other objectives (such as the maintenance of Balance of Trade equilibrium), is the attainment of normal full capacity use. That is, in the long run, the government will always want to avoid both Keynesian unemployment (under-capacity working) and excess aggregate demand (over-capacity working), although the achievement of this and of its other long run objectives will usually entail departures from normal full capacity use in the short run, to which firms will become accustomed. In other words, the government will use fiscal measures in such a way as to counteract autonomous deviations from the equilibrium growth path and to maintain the economy in a state of long run equilibrium (in the particular sense in which we are using the term).

This is not to say that every company will be in equilibrium, for at any given time, no matter how skilful the government's demand management, there are bound to be some companies whose long run expectations are nothing like fulfilled. Nor is it to say that long run equilibrium will prevail continuously, for even at its best the fiscal response to disequilibrium cannot be instantaneous. And it should certainly not be supposed that fiscal stabilisation policy is either simple or error-proof. Nonetheless, demand management of this kind, coupled with the sort of inherent stability discussed earlier, does provide a general reason for believing that in practice modern capitalist economies will normally be sufficiently close to long run equilibrium to make our equilibrium model of the determination of the share of profits an acceptable description of reality.

To the extent that this is not the case, we ought to supplement the equilibrium model with a description of the way in which companies in aggregate respond to nonfulfilment of their expectations. However, we shall not enter into a detailed discussion of disequilibrium, largely because the multiplicity of possible disequilibrium states makes it very difficult to draw conclusions which are both simple and general. Instead, we shall proceed on the assumption that the propositions derived from our equilibrium analysis are normally relevant to the real world, bearing in mind that the principles of the equilibrium model provide a basis for ad hoc investigations of particular disequilibrium situations.

(4) So far we have concentrated on the impact of demand management on the relationship between the actual growth rate and the equilibrium growth rate. But fiscal policy can also alter the equilibrium growth rate itself.* This is evident from the equation which determines the equilibrium growth rate, namely

$$g = \frac{l-a}{k-a}$$

because the level of government expenditure influences the size of the autonomous demand variable, a, and the level of taxation affects the proportional leakage, l. This raises a number of possi-

* Although, as Harrod (1939) points out, 'changes in fundamental conditions have opposite effects on the actual rate and the warranted rate'.

bilities, of which we shall consider, at this point, only those which are pertinent in the context of a closed economy.

First, government action with regard to the equilibrium growth rate provides another way in which the economy might adjust to the sort of scarcity of labour discussed at the end of the previous section. For, even if the two mechanisms mentioned there should prove inadequate, the government could avoid disequilibrium by taking steps to prevent the equilibrium growth rate from exceeding the maximum permitted by the availability of labour. Conversely, in a situation of labour surplus, the government might wish to push the equilibrium growth rate to the maximum permitted by the supply of labour, in order to eliminate Marxian unemployment and to promote induced technical progress. If the government were to behave in this fashion, the equilibrium growth rate would in effect be determined by the availability of labour in relation to the pace of labour-augmenting technical progress (i.e. by the natural rate of growth). This would simplify the present model, since it would be possible to explain the equilibrium growth rate without direct reference to the interaction of the multiplier and the accelerator.

Incidentally, this type of governmental behaviour is of interest also because it would render the neo-Keynesian theory of distribution indeterminate (see pp. 13–15, 117, 125 above). For it would eliminate the need for alterations in the share of profits in order to achieve that ratio of savings to national income which is required to bring the equilibrium rate of growth into line with the natural rate of growth. That is to say, even with fixed propensities to save out of profits and other income, appropriate fiscal measures (i.e. an appropriate level of government saving) can reconcile any and all values of the share of profits with any particular ratio of total savings to national income. In this sense, Keynesian fiscal policy, which is entirely consistent with the present theory of the determination of the share of profits, is inconsistent with neo-Keynesian distribution theory.*

* This is true not only of the standard type of neo-Keynesian model but also of Joan Robinson's model and of Kaldor's Neo-Pasinetti mechanism (since appropriate fiscal measures can reconcile any level of the valuation ratio with any particular ratio of savings to national income); see n† on p. 125 above.

4.6 THE INCIDENCE OF PROFITS TAXES

In discussing fiscal policy in the previous section, we dealt only with its effects on the growth rate. But, because taxation is one of the items in the appropriation account (p. 18 above), we know that fiscal policy also affects the share of profits through its influence on the size of the gross retention ratio. For example, a rise in the proportion of profits paid in tax would tend to reduce the gross retention ratio, which, as may be inferred by inspection of the finance function (p. 109 above), would tend to raise the company sector profit margin. We shall now investigate this latter aspect of taxation with a view to deriving some conclusions about the incidence of profits taxes. In order to simplify the exposition we shall continue to assume that the economy is closed and that all output is produced by the company sector. Our conclusions on tax incidence will not be greatly altered by the relaxation of these assumptions in subsequent sections.

For our purposes it is important to distinguish between two sorts of taxes on profits, namely (i) 'corporation taxes', by which we shall mean taxes to which industrial and commercial companies are liable, and (ii) 'personal taxes', by which we shall mean taxes to which the individual owners of industrial and commercial company securities (apart from industrial and commercial companies themselves) are liable. These labels are slightly inappropriate in that not all of the industrial and commercial company securities which are not owned by industrial and commercial companies belong directly to persons. In particular, a significant proportion is indirectly owned by persons via pension funds, life assurance companies, investment trusts, banks and other institutions, some of which are liable to corporation tax in the ordinary sense. In addition, a small number of industrial and commercial company securities is owned by governmental agencies of various kinds.

It should also be noted that we shall treat as a personal tax any part of a corporation tax which is credited by the tax authority against the tax liability of individual shareholders. In particular, we shall define dividends gross and corporation tax net of all personal taxes, including that part of corporation tax which is imputed to individual shareholders under certain company tax systems. Moreover, we shall treat investment grants from the government as negative corporation taxes, since they are fundamentally indistinguishable from depreciation allowances.

Throughout this section we shall assume that, whatever the government does by way of taxing profits, it adjusts the other aspects of its fiscal policy in such a way as to keep a constant pressure of aggregate demand and thus that the economy is maintained in equilibrium at a constant rate of growth. In addition, we shall assume provisionally that the investment coefficient and the payout ratio (the ratio of dividends to dividends plus retained earnings) are unaffected by taxation. Under these assumptions it is simple to show that corporation taxes on industrial and commercial companies are completely shifted; for example, an increase of £x million in the aggregate corporation tax bill (whether accomplished by a rise in tax rates or by a reduction in investment grants or in the generosity of the allowances made in the calculation of taxable income) will cause an increase of exactly £x million in the aggregate profits of the company sector.

This conclusion (which, incidentally, is consistent with a good deal of empirical evidence)* follows ineluctably from the central principle of the present theory, which is that in the long run profits are determined by the need to finance company sector investment. In particular, the level of net of tax profits (i.e. gross profits minus corporation tax payments) is governed by, and is by definition equal to, the sum of internal finance, dividends and (gross) interest payments, minus (gross) non-trading income,† all of which, under the present assumptions, are determined independently of corporation taxes. In consequence, corporation taxes merely cause the level of (gross) profits to be greater than it would otherwise have been by exactly the amount of the corporation tax payments.

To see why this is so, let us first consider in more detail the consequences of a change in the level of corporation tax from a macroeconomic viewpoint. Since the growth rate and the investment coefficient remain the same, so must the level of investment. Moreover, since the financial asset ratio and the external finance

* See, for example, Krzyzaniak and Musgrave (1963) and Coutts, Godley and Nordhaus (1975).

† This follows directly from the appropriation account identity on p. 18 above.

ratio are also unchanged, so must be the necessary amount of internal finance. In addition, the level of dividends remains constant, because no change takes place either in the payout ratio or in the extent of retained earnings (i.e. internal finance minus depreciation provisions, both of which are unaltered).* Nor does the change in taxation affect (gross) non-trading income or (gross) interest payments, since the level of investment, the liquidity ratio, the gearing ratio and the interest rate are all unchanged. Thus, since no change occurs in any of the determinants of net of tax profits, the only way in which a change in the tax bill can be absorbed is by an equal change in the level of (gross) profits.

In order to understand how the necessary change in profits comes about, we must also examine the process by which corporation taxes are passed on from a microeconomic viewpoint. At the level of the individual firm, an increase (say) in the proportion of profits paid in corporation tax would manifest itself as an adverse shift of the finance frontier. It is clear from the model presented in the previous chapter that this would cause an increase in the firm's profit margin, which, other things being equal, would in turn cause it to lose ground in the competitive struggle for demand and to suffer a lower growth rate. But other things are not equal, because the finance frontiers of all its competitors have also shifted adversely, which will cause them to increase their profit margins, which will cause a favourable shift of the opportunity frontier of the individual firm in question. That is, the firm will discover that it can now achieve any given rate of growth at a higher level of the profit margin than before. Indeed, since the aggregate growth rate of demand is unchanged, the improvement in the opportunity frontier of the representative or average firm will exactly offset the deterioration in its finance frontier in the sense that its chosen growth rate will be unaltered. And provided that its payout ratio and its investment coefficient remain constant, its profits will exceed their former level by exactly the amount by which its corporation tax liability has increased.

It is worth emphasising that the last two sentences apply

* Depreciation provisions (which should not be confused with depreciation allowances for tax purposes) are unaltered because the level of investment and the accounting rules for depreciation are unchanged.

specifically to the representative firm rather than to any arbitrarily selected individual firm. For an across-the-board increase in profit margins caused by a rise in corporation tax will to some extent alter the composition of demand (for example, by changing relative prices; see p. 122 above). In consequence, the shifts in the finance frontier and the opportunity frontier will not in all cases exactly offset one another. Some firms will suffer reductions in their growth rates, and thus their profits will increase by less than their corporation tax liability, the remainder of the extra tax bill being met by reduced investment and dividends, together with certain lesser changes in non-trading income and interest payments. Other firms will achieve higher growth rates than before, and thus their profits will increase by more than their corporation tax bill, the excess of profits being devoted primarily to additional investment and dividends.*

Needless to say, the present analysis of tax incidence presumes that the representative firm is in general reasonably close to long run equilibrium. Even so, the shifting of corporation taxes will not occur instantaneously; a year or two may elapse before firms can fully adjust their long run plans in response to an unanticipated change in taxation. Moreover, we have assumed that a constant pressure of aggregate demand is maintained. If, however, as is commonly the case, the government were to alter the rate of growth at the same time as changing the burden of taxation on profits, this would complicate the analysis by introducing an additional source of change in the level of profits.

So far we have assumed that the size of the payout ratio is unaffected by corporation taxes. In the light of our earlier discussion of the determination of the payout ratio, this assumption is justifiable, provided that the corporation tax system discriminates neither in favour of nor against dividends, or, in other words, provided that the amount of corporation tax paid by a company is independent of its payout ratio (see section 2.4 above, especially pp. 42, 46 and 51). This is true of the current (1975) U.S. tax system. It is not true, though, of the current U.K. tax system (since

---

* Incidentally, implicit in our discussion of the incidence of taxation is the general simplifying assumption made on p. 106 above that induced changes in the relative sizes of individual companies have no systematic effects on the values of aggregate (i.e. weighted average) variables such as the external finance ratio.

we have excluded the shareholder's tax credit from the definition of corporation tax).

If corporation taxes affect the size of the payout ratio, such taxes will not be exactly shifted. If, for example, the corporation tax system were to discriminate against dividends, the payout ratio would be lower than it would otherwise have been, which would result in corporation taxes being less than completely shifted. That is, a certain proportion of the corporation tax bill would be met by a reduction in the level of dividends below what it would otherwise have been rather than by an increase in profits. If, on the other hand, the corporation tax system were to discriminate in favour of dividends, the payout ratio would be higher than would otherwise have been the case, which would lead to corporation taxes being more than completely shifted. That is, profits would be higher than they would otherwise have been by enough not only to cover the corporation tax bill but also to provide additional dividends.

The preceding argument takes it for granted that the external finance ratio is unaffected by corporation taxes. But since interest payments are an allowable deduction for tax purposes, changes in the corporation tax rate might cause changes (in the same direction) in the gearing ratio and thus in the external finance ratio, which would affect the incidence of corporation taxes.* However, if the reasoning on pages 28–32 above is correct, one would expect the effect of changes in the corporation tax rate on the gearing ratio to be slight. For the gearing limit is governed primarily by fears about what would happen in the event of (gross) profits being very low, in which case a company's tax liability would anyway be zero or very small.

The incidence of personal taxes, particularly taxes on dividends and capital gains, is very different from the incidence of corporation taxes. Most notably, if it were the case that personal taxes had no effect on the payout ratio, such taxes would not be shifted at all. This too follows directly from the central principle of the present theory. For the extent of (gross of tax) dividends

---

* For example, an increase in the tax rate would reduce the levels of internal finance, retained earnings and dividends, which would tend to cause corporation taxes to be less than completely shifted. But this effect would be offset by an increase in the level of interest payments, to an extent which depends on a condition similar to that at the end of n† on p. 166 below.

depends only on the payout ratio and on the level of retained earnings (which also affects the extent of gross of tax capital gains on ordinary shares). And the aggregate retained earnings of the company sector depend only on the rate of growth, the investment coefficient, the financial asset ratio, the external finance ratio and the accounting rules for depreciation, none of which is affected by personal taxes.* Thus if personal taxes on dividends and capital gains had no influence on the payout ratio, they would affect neither the extent of (gross of tax) dividends nor the extent of (gross of tax) capital gains. In consequence, the actual incidence of personal taxes would correspond exactly with their nominal incidence.

Things are slightly more complicated if the personal tax system discriminates between dividends and capital gains in the particular sense that the expected total personal tax liability of the shareholder is dependent on the size of the payout ratio (see pp. 46 and 51 above). It remains true that personal taxes will have no effect on the aggregate level of retained earnings. But they will affect the level of dividends by influencing the payout ratio. In particular, if the personal tax system were to discriminate against dividends, personal taxes would be negatively shifted. For the payout ratio and hence the level of (gross of tax) dividends would be lower than they would otherwise have been, without any compensating increase in retained earnings or capital gains, and thus the total cost of personal taxes to shareholders would exceed the amount of personal taxes actually paid. If, by contrast, the personal tax system were to discriminate in favour of dividends, personal taxes would be (positively) shifted to some extent. For the payout ratio and thus the level of (gross of tax) dividends would be higher than would otherwise have been the case, without any offsetting reduction in retained earnings or capital gains, and therefore the total cost of personal taxes to shareholders would be less than the amount of personal taxes actually paid.

It remains to consider one other assumption that we have

---

* Retained earnings are equal to internal finance minus depreciation provisions. The level of internal finance is determined by the amount of investment (which depends on the growth rate and the investment coefficient), the financial asset ratio and the external finance ratio. The level of depreciation provisions depends on the amount of investment and the accounting rules for depreciation.

maintained throughout our discussion of tax incidence, namely
that the investment coefficient is unaffected by taxation. This is
reasonable enough as far as personal taxes and changes in the
rate of corporation tax are concerned.* It is less reasonable with
regard to changes in investment grants and the generosity of depreciation allowances, which effectively alter the price of capital
goods in relation to the prices of other inputs, particularly labour.
Thus, for instance, an increase in the aggregate corporation tax
bill accomplished by a reduction in depreciation allowances will
tend to cause a reduction in the investment coefficient.† In consequence, the increase in corporation tax will be only partially
shifted, even if the payout ratio remains unaltered. In effect, part
of the additional tax liability will be met by a reduction of investment, as opposed to an increase in profits. Similarly, a reduction
of corporation tax brought about by an increase in investment
grants would cause an increase in the investment coefficient. Thus
the resultant fall in aggregate profits would be smaller than the
reduction in the aggregate corporation tax bill.

4.7 THE INFLUENCE OF OTHER SECTORS

In this section we shall very briefly examine the implications of
relaxing our earlier assumption that all output is produced by
the company sector (although we shall continue to assume that
the economy is closed). For in modern capitalist economies, a substantial fraction of national income arises in other sectors, particularly in the public sector (i.e. central and local government and
nationalised industries) and in the unincorporated business sector.‡ In the U.K., for example, only 60 per cent of the output of
the economy is produced by the company sector. This complicates
the present theory of the determination of the share of profits, but
does not significantly alter its substance.

* Provided that we continue to abstract from the type of 'endogenous'
influences on the investment coefficient discussed in section 4.3 above.
† This tendency can be discerned in the empirical conclusions of King (1972),
who also discovers that tax rates as such have no perceptible effect on investment.
‡ One must also take account of such things as the output of financial companies (see p. 2 above) and the convention of treating the imputed rent
of owner-occupied dwellings as a component of national income.

One consequence of the existence of other sectors is that, contrary to what we have so far assumed, the share of profits in national income (which we shall label $\hat{\pi}$) is not the same thing as the company sector profit margin (which we shall continue to label π). The relationship between them is in one sense very simple; it is given by the formula $\hat{\pi} = \phi\pi$, where ϕ is the share of company sector output in national income. Since the company sector normally accounts for less than the whole of national income, the share of profits in national income is normally smaller than the company sector profit margin. Moreover, changes in the share of company sector output over time can (and do) cause substantial changes in the share of profits in national income.

To provide a full explanation of the determination of the share of company sector output in national income and of its behaviour over time is beyond the scope of this book. It depends on a large number of things, including the scope of government activities, the extent of nationalisation, the relative importance of industry and agriculture and the legal and fiscal advantages of incorporation. It also depends on the pattern of demand and in particular on the level of demand for company sector products in relation to the products of other sectors. And in so far as the products of other sectors are substitutable for those of the company sector, the pattern of demand will be affected by the size of the company sector profit margin, although this influence on the share of company sector output in national income is likely to be small by comparison with the influence of other, exogenous, factors.

The introduction of other sectors also requires certain modifications to be made to our account of the determination of the growth rate of company sector output. The principles of the multiplier-accelerator process involved, and thus the form of the equation which determines the equilibrium growth rate, are unaffected, but we must now include autonomous demand for company sector output from other sectors and from households whose incomes arise in other sectors – for example, intermediate goods purchased by nationalised industries and consumer goods purchased by civil servants. Similarly, we must incorporate leakages in the form of expenditure on the output of other sectors – for example, purchases of electricity from a nationalised industry both by companies and by households whose incomes arise in the company sector.

However, we must also recognise that this sort of expenditure on the output of other sectors indirectly generates a certain amount of demand for company sector output by increasing the level of activity in other sectors. For this reason, the existence of other sectors makes it more difficult to establish what part of the demand for company sector output is autonomous and what part is induced. In addition, to the extent that there is substitutability between company sector products and the products of other sectors, both autonomous and induced demand for company sector output, and thus the rate of growth of the company sector, will be affected by the size of the company sector profit margin, although, as we have already suggested, the magnitude of this effect is likely to be comparatively small.

Furthermore, company sector employment is no longer the same thing as employment in the economy as a whole, and thus the supply of labour to the company sector depends not only on the size of the economy's labour force but also on the level of employment in other sectors. For example, even in the absence of Marxian unemployment, the level of employment in the company sector could grow faster than the labour force if other sectors were to shrink. Conversely, a rapid growth of employment in other sectors could cause labour scarcity in the company sector even if the demand for labour in the company sector were increasing more slowly than the economy's labour force.

It remains true that, as we explained in section 4.4 above, there exists no mechanism which would tend automatically to raise the company sector's demand for labour in the event of its being less than the supply. But it is no longer necessarily true that an excess supply of labour in the company sector will be reflected in Marxian unemployment. For, even if we neglect the possibility of government intervention, surplus labour might be absorbed in agriculture, in domestic service or in self-employment in the service sector, in all of which the demand for labour is fairly elastic with respect to the level of the wage. That is, an excess supply of labour in the economy as a whole might drive down the wage rate in these other sectors to the point where the entire labour force is employed.

If this is to happen, however, the wage rate in these other sectors cannot in general be equal to, and must be flexible relative to, the wage rate in the company sector. This is in contrast to, say, orthodox neoclassical multisectoral models, in which wage rates in all sectors are presumed to tend to equality. But in the present model, if there were forces which maintained equal wage rates in all sectors of the economy, or even constant wage differentials between sectors, then there could be no automatic tendency for Marxian unemployment to be eliminated, since wage rates in all sectors would be fixed in terms of company sector products by the need for profits to be such as to finance company sector investment. (Naturally, this would not preclude the government from taking action to reduce Marxian unemployment by raising the growth rate of the economy or increasing the amount of public sector employment.)

Thus, to digress slightly, industrialisation in an economy with flexible relative wages might proceed in something like the following way. Initially, the company sector (which we may roughly identify with the industrial sector) is small, and an excess supply of labour in the company sector causes the equilibrium wage rate in industry to exceed the equilibrium wage rate in the non-industrial sectors by a considerable margin. The relatively high wage in the industrial sector causes the supply of labour to the industrial sector to be infinitely elastic, although the economy's labour force is more or less fully employed. Over time, the industrial sector grows more rapidly than the economy as a whole, sucking labour from the non-industrial sectors; in consequence, the gap between industrial and non-industrial wage rates diminishes. Eventually, the gap becomes so small that a situation of labour scarcity tends to develop in the industrial sector, which cannot be alleviated by further automatic changes in relative wages.*

Finally, the existence of other sectors may affect the incidence of taxes, particularly corporation taxes. For since the economy and

---

* Since there is no mechanism by which the scarcity of labour in the industrial sector can raise the wage rate in the non-industrial sectors above that in the industrial sector, which is what would be necessary in order to induce the non-industrial sectors to release labour. However, this sort of scarcity of labour could be alleviated if the government were to raise the cost of labour in the non-industrial sectors by imposing a payroll tax such as the Selective Employment Tax. It could also be alleviated in the ways discussed on pp. 127–8 above.

the company sector are not one and the same thing, it is no longer strictly valid to assume, as we did in the previous section, that the maintenance of a constant pressure of aggregate demand is sufficient to ensure that the growth rate of the company sector remains unchanged. In particular, for the reasons mentioned above, alterations in the size of the company sector profit margin might have an effect on the growth rate of the company sector relative to the growth rate of the economy as a whole. In consequence, corporation taxes might not be exactly shifted even if the growth rate of the economy, the payout ratio and the investment coefficient were unaffected by taxation.

Consider, for example, an increase in corporation tax, which leads companies to raise their profit margins. The resultant increase in the company sector profit margin might cause a reduction in the growth rate of the company sector, which would in turn cause the aggregate profits of the company sector to rise by less than the increase in the aggregate corporation tax bill, the remainder of the additional tax bill being met primarily by a reduction in investment and dividends. However, we have already argued that the degree of substitutability between company sector products and the products of other sectors is likely to be small. Thus the practical importance of this modification to our earlier analysis of the incidence of corporation taxes is probably not very great.

4.8 FOREIGN TRADE AND MIGRATION

At this point it is convenient to abandon our assumption that the economy is closed and to examine the impact of international economic relationships on the share of profits. For the time being, though, we shall continue to assume that there are no multinational companies.

In many respects, the introduction of foreign trade makes little difference to our model. Exports constitute a further source of autonomous demand for the products of the company sector, and imports are another type of leakage. But, from the point of view of the company sector, exports and imports are fundamentally indistinguishable from sales to and purchases from other domestic sectors (which were discussed in the previous section). From the point of view of the economy as a whole, however, and most notably from the point of view of the government, there is an important difference between foreign and domestic trade. For the government of an open economy cannot disregard the Balance of Trade; in particular, it will seek to prevent the Balance of Trade falling below some target value determined by various considerations relating to long term capital inflows and outflows. As a result, foreign trade may exercise an important indirect influence on the growth rate (and thus on the share of profits) through its effects on fiscal policy.

To illustrate this, let us assume for simplicity that the target value of the Balance of Trade is zero. Let us also assume provisionally that the economy's average propensity to import remains constant over time, which implies that imports grow at the same proportional rate as national income. If this is so, it is clear that in the long run the government cannot allow the growth rate of national income to exceed the growth rate of exports. Similarly, the growth rate of national income could be permitted to exceed the growth rate of exports if the propensity to import were diminishing, and the growth rate of national income would have to be less than the growth rate of exports if the propensity to import were increasing.*

As is well known, the achievement of the government's Balance of Trade target may conflict with the achievement of its other policy objectives, such as the reduction of Marxian unemployment. This would be the case if (a) the government were unable to exercise effective control over the growth rate of exports and the propensity to import (for example, by varying the exchange rate or imposing taxes and subsidies) and (b) the maximum growth rate permitted by the Balance of Trade were less than that which the government would otherwise desire. In such circumstances, the growth rate of the economy, and thus the growth rate of the company sector, would be determined by the behaviour of exports and of the propensity to import rather than by the considerations discussed in earlier sections. This would make our model of the

* Formally, let the minimum acceptable level of the Balance of Trade be some constant proportion (not necessarily zero) of the value of exports, and let the Balance of Trade initially take on its target value. To maintain this target the government must ensure that the growth rate of national income does not exceed $(g_E - g_m)$, where g_E is the growth rate of exports and g_m is the proportional rate of change of the average propensity to import.

determination of the share of profits slightly more complicated because, since foreign products are substitutable for company sector products, the growth rate of exports and the propensity to import are both affected by the size of the company sector profit margin. In particular, any force which tended to increase the company sector profit margin would be offset to some extent by the fact that an increase in the company sector profit margin would reduce the growth rate of exports and increase the propensity to import, which would cause a decrease in the growth rate of the economy.*

It is worth emphasising that the comments in the preceding paragraph relate specifically to the equilibrium growth rate. That is, although a slow rate of growth of exports might prevent the government from eliminating Marxian unemployment, there is no reason why, in the long run, the achievement of the government's Balance of Trade target should conflict with its objective of maintaining normal full capacity use (see p. 131 above). For operating above full capacity, by creating bottlenecks in domestic supply, has an adverse effect on the Balance of Trade by pushing up the propensity to import. Operating below full capacity, on the other hand, has no correspondingly beneficial effect on the propensity to import and the Balance of Trade, and is wasteful in that it unnecessarily reduces the productivity of investment and thus the level of consumption per head. In consequence, even if the rate of growth is constrained by the Balance of Trade, it is still reasonable to suppose that the government will endeavour to manage demand in such a way as to maintain the company sector in a state of long run equilibrium.†

In the context of an open economy, we should also consider the relevance of migration to our earlier discussion of the supply of labour. For emigration provides an additional means by which

---

* For, given that firms behave in the way described in the previous chapter (and in particular that they are sales revenue maximisers), an increase in the company sector profit margin will always tend to cause a decrease rather than an increase in company sector sales revenue.

† Similarly, if, in the long run, the government wanted to cause excess supply in the labour market with a view to reducing wage inflation, the creation of Marxian unemployment (i.e. a reduction in the equilibrium growth rate) would be a less wasteful method than the creation of Keynesian unemployment (i.e. a reduction in the degree of capacity use).

Marxian unemployment might be reduced and immigration provides an additional means by which labour scarcity might be alleviated.* In particular, since governments tend to want as high a growth rate as possible for reasons of national power and prestige, the availability of immigrant labour would make it more likely that the growth rate would be pushed up to the maximum permitted by the Balance of Trade. If, in addition, the government were able to control the growth rate of exports and the propensity to import, its choice of a growth rate might be constrained neither by the availability of labour nor by the Balance of Trade. In such a situation, the effective upper limit on (and hence the determinant) of the growth rate of the economy would probably be the government's inhibitions about the adverse social consequences of too much immigration and the adverse environmental consequences of too large a population.

The existence of foreign trade has certain implications for the incidence of corporation taxes. In circumstances in which the growth rate of the economy is determined by something other than Balance of Trade considerations, no modification is required to our earlier conclusion that, in the absence of induced changes in the payout ratio, the investment coefficient and the share of company sector output in national income, corporation taxes will be completely shifted. But it is of interest to ask to what extent they are shifted on to domestic residents and to what extent on to foreigners. This depends on the proportion of company sector output that is exported and on the degree of substitutability between company sector products and foreign products. The smaller the proportion of exports, and the greater the degree of substitutability, the greater will be the proportion of domestic corporation tax that is shifted on to domestic residents.

Consider, for example, an increase in corporation tax, which leads companies to raise their profit margins. If foreign products are substitutable for company sector products, this will cause a contraction in (foreign and domestic) demand for company sector output. To maintain the growth of the economy at a constant rate, let us suppose that the government takes fiscal steps to increase

* Indeed, in a limiting case, every unemployed worker might emigrate and immigrants might be willing and able to fill every vacancy, which would render the concept of the natural rate of growth of the economy meaningless.

domestic demand for company sector output by an equal amount. Thus the proportion of company sector output which is exported will fall and the proportion of corporation tax which is passed on to domestic residents will rise. Effectively the same result would occur if the government were to react by reducing the exchange rate in order to stimulate (foreign and domestic) demand for company sector output. In this case, however, an increased proportion of corporation tax would be passed on to domestic residents in an indirect way, through the increase in the domestic price of imported goods.

The incidence of corporation taxes is a somewhat more involved subject in circumstances in which the growth rate of the economy is determined by Balance of Trade considerations, because, as we have already mentioned, the growth rate of exports and the propensity to import are likely to depend to some degree on the size of the company sector profit margin. As a result, corporation taxes will be less than completely shifted, to an extent which depends on the degree of substitutability between company sector and foreign products. For example, an increase in the company sector profit margin caused by an increase in corporation tax would cause a decline in the growth rate of the economy and of the company sector. In consequence, the profits of the company sector would increase by less than the addition to the corporation tax bill.

4.9 MULTINATIONAL COMPANIES

Let us now drop the assumption that there are no multinational companies, thus permitting U.K. companies to have foreign subsidiaries and foreign companies to have U.K. subsidiaries. (The analysis in this section is applicable to any country; to simplify the terminology, though, we shall always speak as if the country under consideration were the U.K.). This makes no difference to our theory of the behaviour of the individual firm; the microeconomic model in chapter 3 applies just as well to multinational firms as to firms whose production and marketing facilities are confined to a single country. But the existence of multinational companies does require some modifications to be made to our macroeconomic model of the determination of the share of (company sector) profits in national income.

The main reason for this is that national accountants define 'company sector profits' as profits made by companies in the U.K. and not as the profits of U.K. companies (being companies registered in the U.K. which are not subsidiaries of foreign companies).* That is to say, company sector profits exclude the profits of foreign subsidiaries of U.K. companies and include the profits of U.K. subsidiaries of foreign companies. Similarly, 'company sector investment' is defined not as investment carried out by U.K. companies but as investment carried out by companies in the U.K. That is, it includes investment carried out by U.K. subsidiaries of foreign companies and it excludes investment carried out by foreign subsidiaries of U.K. companies.

In consequence, company sector profits and investment include not only the profits and investment of whole companies but also the profits and investment of parts of companies. The distinction is significant because the foundation of our macroeconomic model is provided by a microeconomic model of the behaviour of whole firms. Indeed, the fact that the firm is a self-contained financial unit, within which there is perfect mobility of funds, is crucial to the present theory. For it was on this basis that we defined and discussed the financial asset ratio, the external finance ratio and the gross retention ratio, three variables which play a fundamental part in all our analysis.

Thus to accommodate multinational companies in our macroeconomic model we must splice the profits and investment of the company sector, which includes only the parts of certain companies, to the profits and investment of some relevant aggregate of whole companies, which, in accordance with national accounting convention, we shall take to be U.K. companies inclusive of their foreign subsidiaries. Two parallel operations are involved:

(1) Splicing the profits of the company sector, which we shall label P, to the profits of U.K. companies, which we shall label $\bar{P}$. The difference between $\bar{P}$ and P we shall call net foreign profits, being the profits of foreign subsidiaries of U.K. companies minus the profits of U.K. subsidiaries of foreign companies. Let net foreign profits be some fraction, $(1-\alpha)$, of the profits of U.K. companies. It follows that† $P = \alpha\bar{P}$, which defines the relation-

* See Maurice (1968).   † Since $\bar{P} - P = (1-\alpha)\bar{P}$.

ship between the profits of the company sector and the profits of U.K. companies.

(2) Splicing the investment of the company sector, which we shall label I, to the investment of U.K. companies, which we shall label $\bar{I}$. The difference between $\bar{I}$ and I we shall call net foreign investment. This is the acquisition by U.K. companies of physical assets abroad (both by capital formation and by the purchase of existing companies) minus the acquisition by foreign companies of physical assets in the U.K. Let net foreign investment be some fraction, $(1-\beta)$, of the investment of U.K. companies. It follows that* $I = \beta \bar{I}$, which defines the connection between company sector investment and the investment of U.K. companies.

The finance function of U.K. companies, which is a relationship between the profits of U.K. companies and the investment of U.K. companies, may be written as

$$\bar{P} = \frac{(1+f-x)}{r}\bar{I}.$$

By using our splicing variables, α and β, we can transform this into a relationship between the profits of the company sector and the investment of the company sector, namely

$$P = \frac{\alpha}{\beta}\frac{(1+f-x)}{r}I,$$

which, when divided through by company sector value added, becomes

$$\pi = \frac{\alpha}{\beta}\frac{(1+f-x)}{r}gk,$$

where π is the company sector profit margin, g is the growth rate of company sector value added and k is the company sector investment coefficient; f, x and r, however, are the financial asset ratio, the external finance ratio and the gross retention ratio of

---

* Since $\bar{I}-I = (1-\beta)\bar{I}$. Incidentally, the net acquisition of financial assets by industrial and commercial companies, in the sense in which this phrase is used in the British national accounts, is now $(1-\beta+f-x)\bar{I}$ or $((1+f-x)/\beta-1)I$. When net foreign investment is zero (i.e. when $\beta = 1$), both these terms reduce to $(f-x)I$; see n * on p. 105 above.

U.K. companies.* This last equation, which is simply another version of the finance function, replaces the version of the finance function which was introduced at the beginning of this chapter (p. 109 above). The remainder of the macroeconomic argument, which is concerned principally with the way in which the company sector growth rate and investment coefficient are determined, then follows as before.

It is clear from the last equation that the existence of multinational companies normally affects the size of the company sector profit margin and hence the size of the share of profits in national income. Other things being equal, the greater are net foreign profits, the smaller will be α (the ratio of company sector profits to U.K. company profits) and thus the smaller will be the company sector profit margin. This is because a greater proportion of investment is financed out of foreign profits, which means that domestic profits can be lower than would otherwise have been necessary. Similarly, other things being equal, the greater is net foreign investment, the smaller will be β (the ratio of company sector investment to U.K. company investment) and thus the larger will be the company sector profit margin. This is because a larger proportion of profits is devoted to the financing of foreign investment, and therefore a higher level of profits is necessary in order to finance any given level of domestic investment.

These examples show that net foreign profits and net foreign investment act in opposite directions on the share of profits. More precisely, it is apparent from the last equation that what is important as far as the impact of multinational companies on the share of profits is concerned is not the sizes of α and β individually, but their sizes relative to one another, which governs the value of the ratio α/β. In other words, if the extent of net foreign profits were very different from the extent of net foreign investment,

---

* Thus all the elements of the appropriation account, the sources of funds account and the uses of funds account (pp. 18–19 above) relate to U.K. companies rather than to the company sector. With reference to these accounts, though, it should be noted (a) that interest and dividend payments by U.K. companies may be made to both U.K. and overseas residents, (b) that U.K. companies may acquire financial assets in the U.K. or overseas, (c) that the non-trading income of U.K. companies may arise in the U.K. or overseas, (d) that U.K. companies may pay taxes to both the U.K. and overseas governments and (e) that U.K. companies may raise external finance either in the U.K. or overseas.

α and β would differ widely in size and their combined influence on the company sector profit margin would be considerable. If, by contrast, the ratio of net foreign profits to company sector profits were equal to the ratio of net foreign investment to company sector investment, α and β would be equal and the ratio α/β would be unity, which would cause net foreign profits and net foreign investment to have no influence on the share of profits. This is significant because net foreign profits and net foreign investment are not independently determined. Indeed, because a high level of net foreign profits is both a result and a cause of a high level of net foreign investment, α and β tend to be similar in size in any particular country, which implies that in practice their separate influences on the share of profits tend to cancel one another out.*

To give a full account of the determination of net foreign profits and net foreign investment would be a lengthy exercise. As we have already suggested, the extent of net foreign profits depends on what net foreign investment has been in the past, and on the profitability of the U.K. subsidiaries of foreign companies in relation to the profitability of the foreign subsidiaries of U.K. companies (which in turn has an effect on the current level of net foreign investment). The extent of net foreign investment, past and present, and the profitability (both for U.K. and for foreign companies) of locating production and marketing facilities in the U.K. rather than in other countries, depends on many different factors. These include (1) the availability and cost of various sorts of raw materials, (2) the availability and cost of labour, (3) the location of markets, (4) transportation costs, (5) the advantages of intra-company (as distinct from inter-company) transactions in the several sorts of inputs and outputs and (6) political and legal constraints and incentives (including tax advantages).†

Net foreign profits and net foreign investment are likely to be

* They would exactly offset one another in a steady state (i.e. when net foreign investment is a constant proportion of company sector investment over time) in which, on average, U.K. companies earned the same rate of profit on foreign and domestic capital and in which the U.K. subsidiaries of foreign companies earned the same average profit rate as U.K. companies.

† See, for example, ch. III and other parts of Reddaway et al. (1967, 1968).

affected by various forces which also influence the share of profits in other ways. For example, net foreign investment would probably be increased by labour scarcity and diminished by Marxian unemployment or by the fact of a large proportion of the labour force being employed in non-industrial sectors. Moreover, the extent of net foreign investment may depend on the share of profits itself, which influences the level of the real wage in the company sector. But the behaviour of net foreign profits and net foreign investment is governed primarily by forces unrelated to the share of profits. Thus, as a first approximation to reality, and bearing in mind that it is the extent of the difference between them that is important, it would not be unreasonable to treat net foreign profits and net foreign investment as if they were strictly exogenously determined.

The existence of multinational companies makes the subject of the incidence of corporation taxes somewhat more complicated. To begin with, despite the prevalence of double taxation agreements of various kinds, the amount of tax paid by any given company is liable to depend on the tax systems and tax rates of more than one country. Furthermore, the 'geographical' incidence of corporation taxes will depend not only on the pattern of international trade in company products but also on the international distribution of the production and marketing facilities of the companies of any given nationality.

But the essence of our earlier conclusions on tax incidence remains the same; in particular, the analysis of corporation tax shifting in a single closed economy also applies directly to the world as a whole. Let us assume, for instance, that no change occurs in the growth rate of the world economy, in the share of company output in total world output, in the average payout ratio or in the average investment coefficient. In this case, corporation taxes would be completely shifted; an increase of $£x$ million in the aggregate tax bill of all the companies in the world would cause an $£x$ million increase in their aggregate profits.

However, what is true for all the companies in the world is not necessarily true for any individual subgroup such as U.K. companies. For an increase in the effective rate of corporation tax on U.K. companies relative to foreign companies would lead U.K. companies to raise their profit margins relative to foreign companies, which would cause a reduction in the growth rate of U.K. companies and a corresponding increase in the growth rate of foreign companies.* Thus the profits of U.K. companies would rise by less than the amount of the increase in their tax bills; the difference, however, would (under the present assumptions) be made up exactly by an increase in the profits of foreign companies (over and above any increase in their tax bills). This, incidentally, would affect the share of profits in U.K. national income by altering net foreign profits and net foreign investment (i.e. by changing α and β). Specifically, an increase in corporation taxes on U.K. companies, by reducing their share in world (and in U.K. company sector) output, would reduce net foreign investment, which would tend to depress the share of profits. However, it is probable that this tendency would be offset to some extent by a fall in net foreign profits.†

* It might also cause U.K. companies to transform themselves into foreign companies.

† This is not necessarily true. Since U.K. companies would be selling less than before, but at a higher profit margin, it is possible that their share of total world profits might increase and thus net foreign profits might rise.

5

SOME IMPLICATIONS FOR
GOVERNMENT POLICY

To understand the way in which the economy works is a legitimate end in itself. But the significance of economic theory derives ultimately from its capacity to influence social behaviour. Thus it is appropriate to conclude by drawing out some of the implications of the present theory of profits for government policy, with particular reference to measures aimed at improving the distribution of income.

Without entering into a full discussion of the principles of distributive justice, it may be noted that there are two reasons why a concern with fairness might lead one to wish to reduce the share of profits in national income. The first is that the ownership of capital, since it involves very little work, is an inadequate moral basis for receiving income which would otherwise accrue to wage and salary earners. The second is that the ownership of company sector capital (i.e. company securities) is so highly concentrated that a reduction in the share of profits would make the distribution of income among persons significantly less unequal and would therefore cause income to be distributed more nearly in accordance with needs.*

Moral sentiments of this kind are widely held. But governments of all complexions have been inhibited in giving expression to them by the belief that profits and investment are intimately associated and in consequence by the fear that measures which improve the distribution of income may adversely affect employ-

* That company securities are the most unequally distributed type of personal wealth can be seen from the studies of Lydall and Tipping (1961) and Lampman (1962); in the U.K. in 1954, for example, 96 per cent of company securities was owned by the wealthiest 5 per cent of the population. It is of course true that a significant proportion of company securities is also held by pension funds and life assurance companies, but it must be recognised that for the most part these provide the pensions of people who are relatively rich. In particular, personal interests in these institutional holdings are probably much less equally distributed than wages and salaries.

ment and productivity growth. These fears are not without foundation. But policy making in this area has been severely handicapped by a very imperfect understanding of the nature of the causal connection between profits and investment, which has made it almost impossible to assess the likely effects of particular measures either on the distribution of income or on the level of investment.

The present theory, however, is in effect a precise specification of the nature of the linkage between profits and investment. Thus it enables one to predict the probable consequences of alternative policies, which is a necessary precondition of making rational choices between them. Not least, the present theory implies that certain widely advocated measures are either ineffectual or inefficient. More importantly, it also implies that there are ways in which the distribution of income might be made more equitable without any adverse influence on investment. We shall pursue these various implications in the simplest possible way, namely by analysing the effects of a series of specific policy measures in the light of the present theory. Before doing this, though, some preliminary points must be made.

First, not all of profits (in the sense in which we are using the word) is significant from the point of view of the fairness of income distribution. Dividends and interest are evidently relevant because they accrue directly to the owners of company securities. But one should leave out of account all taxes on profits, dividends, interest and capital gains, since they confer no particular benefits on the owners of company securities.* Retained earnings and depreciation provisions pose greater problems. They cannot be totally ignored since, by affecting the value of assets per share, they exercise an indirect influence on share prices and thus on the welfare of shareholders. But it is conventional to regard some part of depreciation provisions and retained earnings as a cost of production rather than as income, and to ignore this part in assessing the impact of profits on the fairness of the distribution of income.

In particular, few people would dispute that at the very least

* Except in so far as the pattern of public expenditure is such as to benefit the rich (who include the owners of most company securities) more than other members of the community. In this connection, it should be borne in mind that we are treating investment grants as negative taxes.

one should leave out of account an allowance for depreciation based on the historical cost of fixed assets, or, in other words, an allowance roughly equal to the amount of expenditure on assets that would be required to preserve intact the money value of a company's capital. Some, however, would maintain that in periods of inflation one should also leave out of account that further part of gross profits which, if spent on assets, would preserve intact the volume of a company's capital (which implies that the allowance for depreciation should be based on the replacement cost rather than the historical cost of fixed assets and that stock appreciation – see p. 111 above – should be deducted from retained earnings). Others in turn have advocated that this sort of allowance for inflation should be based instead on the maintenance of the purchasing power of a company's capital with respect to a wide range of goods.

Which of these various possible approaches is the correct one is an ethical question whose answer depends very largely on conventions about how income should be defined in other contexts. Such conventions vary from time to time and place to place. Therefore, since this point is not crucial to the argument below, we shall sidestep it by treating all retained earnings as relevant from the point of view of the fairness of income distribution and all depreciation provisions as irrelevant, leaving open the question of how depreciation provisions should be calculated and retained earnings measured.

One must also bear in mind that not all industrial and commercial company securities are owned by individual persons. In particular, although the bulk of dividends, interest and capital gains on such securities accrues directly to persons, a substantial proportion accrues indirectly to persons via several sorts of institutions, and a small part accrues to the public sector (see p. 134 above). As a result, the impact of dividends, interest and capital gains on the distribution of income among persons is not entirely straightforward.

In the course of examining the advantages and disadvantages of particular policy measures, we shall accept without question that, other things being equal, it is desirable to reduce the shares of dividends, interest and retained earnings in national income and to make the personal distribution of income more equal in other ways. We shall also accept without question that investment is a desirable activity. In particular, we shall accept that the government is capable of choosing a socially optimal long run growth rate of real national income in the light of labour supply and Balance of Trade considerations, and we shall assume that it ensures by appropriate fiscal policies that aggregate demand grows at this rate. To achieve this growth rate of national income, given the share of the company sector in total output and the company sector investment coefficient, a particular level of company sector investment is required.

It follows from the account of company behaviour presented in earlier chapters that the maintenance of the chosen growth rate of demand is sufficient to cause companies to carry out the required level of investment, provided only that individual companies are free to choose their own profit margins. It also follows that, other things being equal, the attainment of the chosen growth rate of national income will cause the share of profits to be of a particular size. In consequence, the share of profits could always be reduced if the government were prepared to reduce the long run growth rate of aggregate demand and national income. But we shall rule this out as a possible way of improving the distribution of income. That is, we shall accept that the achievement of the chosen growth rate of national income and its associated level of company sector investment is a first priority.

We shall also exclude the possibility of reducing the share of profits by lowering the company sector investment coefficient (i.e. by persuading companies to reduce the rate of replacement of existing capital or the capital intensity of new investment), which would diminish the amount of investment required to sustain any particular growth rate. Indeed, we shall accept that the government may legitimately decide that the investment coefficient ought to be increased in order to raise labour productivity, and that this too takes priority over improvements in the distribution of income.

Let us now investigate the effects of eight specific types of policy measure on the distribution of income and the level of investment. Since the present theory of profits is essentially a long run theory, we shall concentrate exclusively on the long run effects of the policy measures in question and we shall neglect their short run

SOME IMPLICATIONS FOR GOVERNMENT POLICY

effects. We shall also neglect altogether the implications of the present theory of company behaviour for short run policy in general.*

(i) *Corporation taxes*

The incidence of corporation taxes on industrial and commercial companies was discussed at length in the previous chapter (section 4.6 and pp. 143–4, 147 and 153). We concluded that, subject to certain relatively minor qualifications, such taxes are completely shifted. It follows that, contrary to what is commonly supposed, they have very little effect either on the distribution of income or on the level of investment. For example, provided the government maintained a constant pressure of aggregate demand, an increase in the corporation tax bill would have no adverse influence on investment. By the same token, since the level of retained earnings and (given the payout ratio) the level of dividends would remain the same, it would have no beneficial influence on the distribution of income. The principal exceptions to this rule are the following.†

(a) Certain sorts of corporation tax systems discriminate either in favour of or against dividends and thus affect the distribution of income by influencing the payout ratio and the share of dividends in national income, even though they have no effect on the level of investment.

(b) Since the extent of corporation tax liability depends on the generosity of depreciation allowances and investment grants (which we are treating as negative corporation taxes), the corporation tax system may influence the level of investment by affecting the investment coefficient. Since this affects the level of retained

---

* See, however, the discussion in sections 2.2, 3.6 and 4.5 above. Among other things, the present theory implies that varying the availability of short term credit to companies is a highly undesirable method of demand management. For it does not affect the long run level of company sector investment, but merely makes the short run time pattern of investment outlays less smooth, which necessarily destabilises the economy. The present theory also implies that long run investment plans, which are based on expectations of secular trends, are very insensitive to year-to-year changes in the level of aggregate demand (which tends to stabilise the economy). However, large short run changes in the level of demand may affect the amount of investment actually carried out in any particular year through their influence on the short run liquidity position of companies.

† Three other exceptions, which are of little importance in practice, are discussed on pp. 138, 143–4 and 148 above.

earnings and thus of dividends (and indeed of interest payments), it also influences the distribution of income.

For the most part, though, corporation taxes on industrial and commercial companies are in effect simply a peculiar form of sales tax, peculiar because the rate of tax varies in a quite arbitrary way as between one commodity and another. In consequence, a case could be made for abolishing them and replacing them by some other form of indirect taxation, while at the same time retaining an investment grant system as a means of influencing the investment coefficient. For various reasons it might be thought desirable to continue to tax financial companies;* this could be accomplished most easily by abolishing company taxes on trading profits but not on non-trading income or capital gains.

(ii) *Profit sharing*

So many sorts of schemes for making the distribution of income more equitable have been put forward under the general heading of 'profit sharing' that it would be impossible to do them all justice here.† This is particularly true of those whose main object has been to alter the distribution of control in industry. But some grasp of the possibilities and problems in this area may be obtained by considering two different types of profit sharing scheme, which between them incorporate most of the fundamental principles embodied in the various specific proposals alluded to above.

(a) The government obliges every company to pay a fixed percentage of its earnings (i.e. dividends plus retained earnings) to its employees in addition to their wages and salaries. The effects of this would be analogous to those of an increase in the corporation tax rate under a corporation tax system which discriminated neither in favour of nor against dividends. That is, it would cause the finance frontier of every company to deteriorate, which in turn would cause an increase in the company sector profit margin

---

* Not least because financial companies probably do not shift taxes to the same extent as industrial and commercial companies, partly because 'personal taxes' on profits (which we defined as including taxes paid by financial companies) are for the most part not shifted (see pp. 138–9 above), and partly because, as we suggested earlier (p. 8n†), financial companies may behave in a more orthodox way than industrial and commercial companies.
† For an introduction, see Atkinson (1972) pp. 236–48, and the references cited therein.

such as to make the aggregate profits of the company sector greater than they would otherwise have been by exactly the amount of profits paid to employees. In consequence, although this scheme would have no adverse effect on investment, it would not alter the shares of interest, dividends and retained earnings in national income.

A possible variant of this scheme would be to make the employees' share of profits proportional to dividends rather than earnings. This would depress the company sector payout ratio, since it would be similar to the introduction of a corporation tax system which discriminated against dividends. As a result, although this variant would almost certainly cause the share of profits in national income to increase, it would have a beneficial effect on the distribution of income by reducing the share of dividends without increasing the share of retained earnings or affecting the level of investment. A symmetrical variant would be to make the employees' share of profits proportional to retained earnings rather than earnings. This would raise the payout ratio, which would have an adverse effect on the distribution of income by increasing the share of dividends in national income.

It must be stressed, however, that both the basic scheme and its variants would redistribute income among employees in a manner that many people would regard as inequitable. First, there would be an increase in the incomes of company sector employees relative to employees in other sectors, since all employees would suffer from the effects of higher profit margins while only those in the company sector would derive an offsetting benefit in the form of a share of profits. Secondly, within the company sector itself, even if some sort of adjustment were made to compensate for inter-industry differences in the capital–labour ratio, the incomes of the employees of profitable firms would be increased in relation to the incomes of those who happened to be employed in less profitable firms.

In addition, it should be noted that schemes of this type commonly require the employee's share of profits to be saved rather than spent, either for some fixed period or until the employee retires. If such savings were directly or indirectly invested in company sector securities, this would cause the ownership of company sector securities to become less concentrated, which in turn would make the distribution of personal incomes more equal. But this is not a feature which is peculiar to profit sharing schemes; indeed, the same result could be achieved without the inequities mentioned in the preceding paragraph by a scheme of compulsory saving out of wages and salaries.

(b) The government obliges every company to transfer into the ownership of its employees, without charge, a fixed proportion of its retained earnings each year. This might be accomplished by means of a free new issue of ordinary shares to the employees each year.* These shares could be distributed directly to individual employees or held in trust for them by the relevant trade unions.

Provided that the government maintained a constant growth rate of aggregate demand, this sort of scheme would cause no change in the level of investment. However, it is not clear that it would make the distribution of income more equitable; in this regard, three factors must be considered. (1) The free issues of shares to employees would cause the ownership of company sector securities to become less concentrated, which would tend to improve the distribution of income. (2) But these issues would also cause companies to raise their payout ratios. For this sort of scheme, which would divert a proportion of the capital gains on a company's shares from its existing shareholders to its employees, would be analogous in its effects to a change in the tax system which reduced the degree of fiscal discrimination against dividends. Thus there would be an increase in the shares of profits and dividends in national income, which would tend to make the distribution of income less equitable. (3) Finally, this sort of profit sharing scheme, like scheme (a) above, would cause what many would regard as an unfair redistribution of income between different groups of employees.

(iii) *Anti-monopoly policy*

It is an implication of the present theory that measures which attack monopolistic and collusive practices by companies will have little or no effect on the distribution of income (see especially

---

* The size of the new issue relative to the total number of shares outstanding being determined by the size of the employees' proportion of the year's retained earnings relative to the total book value of the equity assets of the company.

pp. 109–10 above). For, although such measures might diminish the share of profits to some slight extent by reducing the share of the company sector in total output, the size of the share of profits depends primarily on the growth rate of national income, the investment coefficient, the external finance ratio, the financial asset ratio and the gross retention ratio, none of which is affected by anti-monopoly policies in any systematic way.

In other respects, however, anti-monopoly policies are both effective and desirable. For monopolistic practices and measures to combat them, despite the fact that they have little effect on the profit margin and the growth rate of the company sector as a whole, undoubtedly have substantial effects on the relative profit margins and growth rates of individual firms. And although we argued earlier that competition and the desire for growth tend (a) to drive the profit margin of every firm down to the minimum financially necessary and (b) to reduce unit costs, it does not follow that unconstrained rivalry between firms would necessarily yield socially optimal results; on the contrary, the exploitation of a monopolistic position by a particular firm or group of firms might well have extremely undesirable effects.

Nor does it follow that it is impossible to make valid judgements that certain sorts of purchasing, pricing and marketing practices should be prohibited because they are counter to the public interest. It is essential, however, that such judgements should be based, not on the relative profitability of the companies concerned, but on the intrinsic nature of the practices themselves. For it should be clear from the microeconomic model developed in chapter 3 that a high rate of profit and a high rate of growth are by no means a sure sign of monopolistic malpractices. Indeed, in reality, differences in profitability between companies are more likely to reflect differences in efficiency of a kind which is socially desirable.

(iv) Restrictions on profit margins
It has sometimes been suggested that the distribution of income would be made more equitable if the government were to impose a permanent upper limit on the size of profit margins. Proposals of this kind have been objected to, quite reasonably, on the grounds that, even if a certain amount of flexibility and administrative

discretion were permitted, they would inevitably bear on different companies in an uneven and arbitrary way, which would be inequitable and would promote inefficiency. But for our purposes it is convenient to assume that some scheme could be devised which overcame these 'microeconomic' objections and to confine our attention to the 'macroeconomic' impact of profit margin restrictions on the distribution of income and the level of investment.

First of all, it is evident that nothing would happen if the statutory upper limit on the company sector profit margin were equal to or greater than the profit margin which would otherwise have prevailed. Let us suppose, however, that the upper limit would be sufficiently low to reduce the company sector profit margin below what it would otherwise have been. The result of such a restriction would be a fall in the level of investment and an improvement in the distribution of income.

The level of company sector investment would be reduced because the imposition of an arbitrary upper limit on a company's profit margin would not cause it to alter its financial policies; in particular, for reasons discussed at length in chapters 2 and 3, the desire of its managers to achieve the highest possible growth rate would already have led them to choose the highest possible external finance ratio and the lowest possible financial asset ratio and payout ratio. As a result, government-imposed restrictions on the company sector profit margin, if they were low enough to be effective, would reduce the availability of finance and would in consequence force a reduction in the level of company sector investment.*

This would have two results. (1) The rate of growth of company sector capacity and output would fall, even if the government were to maintain the same rate of growth of aggregate demand. To some extent the resultant excess demand in the company sector might stimulate output, investment and employment in other

---

* This can be seen at a microeconomic level by inspection of figure 6 (p. 89), which we may suppose relates to the representative firm in the company sector. The government-imposed upper limit on the profit margin, $\pi_{\max}$, can be represented in the diagram by a horizontal line. If $\pi_{\max}$ is greater than π_4, which is the profit margin that the firm would otherwise choose, it will have no effect. If, however, $\pi_{\max}$ were less than π_4, it is clear that it would cause the firm to choose both a lower growth rate and a lower investment coefficient than it would otherwise have done.

domestic sectors. But the degree of substitutability between the products of the company sector and those of other sectors is small, and thus the principal effects of such a fall in the rate of growth of company sector capacity would be a reduction in the rate of growth of national income and the level of employment and a deterioration in the Balance of Trade. (2) The company sector investment coefficient would fall. That is to say, there would be a reduction in the rate of replacement of old plant and equipment and in the capital intensity of new plant and equipment. This would adversely affect the rate of growth of labour productivity.

At the same time, of course, this cut in the level of investment, together with the absence of change in the payout ratio and the gearing ratio, would cause a fall in the shares of profits, dividends, interest and retained earnings in national income. But if the government wished to make such an improvement in the distribution of income by reducing the level of investment, it would be preferable in every respect for it to do so straightforwardly, by lowering the rate of growth of aggregate demand.

(v) *Interest rate policy*

The limited efficacy of the four types of policy measure that we have so far discussed stems in part from one common factor, which is that none of them has any effect on the external finance ratio or the financial asset ratio. For as long as these two ratios remain constant, there is no way in which the level of retained earnings (which governs the level of dividends via the payout ratio) can be reduced without diminishing the level of investment to an equal extent.* It is a corollary of this, though, that any policy measure which caused an increase in the external finance ratio or a decrease in the financial asset ratio would reduce the shares of dividends and retained earnings in national income, which would tend to make the distribution of income more equitable, without any change in the level of investment. In developing policy measures of this kind, however, two problems must be faced.

(1) The fact that the pursuit of growth will already have led managers to maximise the external finance ratio and minimise

---

* Since investment is by definition equal to retained earnings plus depreciation provisions (whose magnitude is in effect exogenously determined) plus external finance minus the acquisition of financial assets.

the financial asset ratio makes it difficult to devise measures which would bring about further increases in the external finance ratio or further decreases in the financial asset ratio. In particular, since the extent of new issues is limited by the reluctance of managers to inflict losses on existing shareholders rather than by any shortage of potential purchasers,* it would not be possible to raise the external finance ratio simply by channelling additional funds into the new issue market. Similarly, since the extent of company borrowing is limited (in the long run) by reluctance to borrow rather than reluctance to lend, to increase the availability of credit would not raise the external finance ratio, although the financial asset ratio might be reduced if the government were to guarantee that in future the rationing of short term credit to companies would not be used as an implement of demand management.

(2) Moreover, an increase in the external finance ratio brought about by an increase in the company sector gearing ratio would enlarge the share of interest payments in national income. This would tend to make the distribution of income less equitable, possibly by enough to offset completely the beneficial influence of the increase in the external finance ratio on the shares of dividends and retained earnings.†

* Because any new issue can be sold, provided the price is low enough. In consequence, a company can always raise additional finance by issuing new shares, as long as its share price remains positive and as long as it is prepared to ignore the interests of its existing shareholders.

† For example, given the identity in n * on p. 165 and the algebraic expressions in the footnotes of section 3.3, and assuming for simplicity (i) that investment in stocks is measured in such a way that stock appreciation (see p. 11 above) is always zero and (ii) that depreciation provisions are calculated on a replacement cost basis, it is possible to show that the combined share of earnings and interest in company sector output is equal in steady state growth to

$$c\{[g_K((1+f')(1-x')-n)-i(x'(1+f')-f')]/(1-\gamma)+ux'(1+f')\},$$

where x' is the gearing ratio, n is the proceeds of new issues as a ratio of net investment, f' is the liquidity ratio, g_K is the constant-price growth rate of company sector physical capital (net of depreciation), i is the proportional rate of increase in the prices of physical assets, c is the company sector physical capital–output ratio (which we shall regard as exogenously determined), γ is the payout ratio and u is the money rate of interest. Whether the value of this expression would be increased or decreased by a rise in the gearing ratio depends on whether u is greater or smaller than $(g_K+i)/(1-\gamma)$.

But there is one way in which the government could solve both these problems – by reducing the interest rate. For a permanent fall in the money rate of interest, by reducing the risks attached to any particular level of the gearing ratio, would encourage companies to raise their gearing ratios, which would increase the external finance ratio and reduce the shares of dividends and retained earnings in national income.* At the same time, such a fall in the interest rate would tend to reduce the share of interest in national income, which would counteract the tendency for an increase in the gearing ratio to enlarge the share of interest. In consequence, the net effect of a reduction in the interest rate would be a diminution of the combined share of dividends, retained earnings and interest in national income.†

In this way the government can in principle, and to a limited extent, alter the fairness of the distribution of income by changing the rate of interest. In practice, its willingness and freedom to do so are likely to be limited by a number of other considerations, not the least of which is the need to maintain the foreign exchange reserves. But it is worth noting that the government's interest rate policy ought not to be influenced by its attitude towards company sector investment. For the present theory implies that changes in the interest rate, although they affect the size of the company sector profit margin, have little or no effect on the level of company sector investment.

* For a discussion of the influence of the money rate of interest on the gearing ratio and hence on the external finance ratio, see pp. 31–2 above (including the footnotes). Changes in the interest rate are unlikely to alter the financial asset ratio. But they will affect the extent of non-trading income, which will influence the share of profits through its effects on the gross retention ratio. This, however, will not affect the shares of dividends, retained earnings or interest in national income.

† It is quite easy to demonstrate this formally. Let us assume for simplicity that the risks of borrowing cause managers to set an upper limit, θ, on the ratio of interest payments to earnings: if this is so, the gearing ratio is determined by the relationship $x' = \theta\rho'/u$, where ρ' is the ratio of earnings to the value of the physical capital stock. This expression for x' can be substituted into the expression for the combined share of earnings and interest presented in the last footnote but one. The first derivative of the resulting expression with respect to the interest rate, u, is positive.

(vi) *Wage restraint*

Governmental control of money wage and salary increases is frequently used and advocated as a means of reducing the rate of inflation of the general price level. It is popularly believed, however, that wage restraint of this sort causes the share of profits in national income to become larger and in consequence causes the distribution of income to become less equitable. It is an implication of the present theory that this belief, while not altogether devoid of truth, is very misleading. For it follows from the argument of earlier chapters that the size of the share of profits, and more particularly the size of the company sector profit margin, is largely independent of the rate of inflation. Moreover, in so far as a reduction in the rate of increase of money wages and salaries would affect the share of profits at all, it is not easy to say whether the net result would be an increase or a decrease in the share of profits. There are in fact four ways in which a fall in the rate of inflation might affect the share of profits.

(a) It might reduce the size of the investment coefficient by reducing the value of investment in stocks. For, as was explained earlier (p. 107), if stocks are valued on a 'first in, first out' basis, some investment in stocks is required in periods of inflation simply to maintain the volume of stocks intact. As a result, a fall in the rate of inflation might tend, in contradiction of the popular belief mentioned, to diminish the shares of profits, dividends and retained earnings in national income.

(b) Furthermore, if companies calculate depreciation provisions on the basis of historical cost (rather than replacement cost) a decrease in the rate of inflation will tend to reduce the share of retained earnings in national income, since it will increase the proportion of investment financed out of depreciation provisions. Given the payout ratio, this would tend to cause a fall in the share of dividends and hence a reduction in the share of profits.

(c) A fall in the rate of inflation might also influence the share of profits by affecting the willingness of companies to borrow. For, given the money interest rate and hence the size of the company sector gearing ratio (see p. 31n), inflation raises the proportion of new investment which companies are prepared to finance by borrowing, since it causes the value of existing physical assets to increase in relation to the value of outstanding debt (see p. 32n). For this reason, a fall in the rate of inflation would tend to reduce the external finance ratio and thus to raise the shares of profits, dividends and retained earnings in national income.* This, however, would be offset in part by a reduction in the financial asset ratio.† Moreover, a fall in the rate of inflation would probably lead to a fall in the money interest rate, which would tend to raise the gearing ratio and the external finance ratio and thus to reduce the share of profits. The net effect of these conflicting tendencies cannot be ascertained *a priori*.

(d) Wage restraint would tend to increase the share of profits if the growth rate of exports or the propensity to import were to depend on the domestic rate of inflation in circumstances in which the growth rate of national income was constrained by Balance of Trade considerations. In such a case, wage restraint, by increasing the growth rate of the economy, would indeed tend to raise the shares of profits, dividends, interest and retained earnings in national income. But, by increasing the level of investment, it would also reduce the amount of unemployment.

(vii) *Dividend restraint*

At various times, and for various reasons, governments have obliged or encouraged companies to keep their dividend payments below what they would otherwise have been. Although most such measures have been temporary, it is of some interest to consider the consequences of a permanent reduction in the company sector payout ratio brought about by means of statutory restriction of dividends.

It is obvious that this would cause a fall in the share of dividends in national income. However, the present theory also implies something less obvious, which is that, contrary to what is commonly

---

* That a reduction in the rate of inflation would tend to increase the combined share of earnings and interest in this way is apparent from the algebraic expression in n † on p. 166 (from which the influence of factors (a) and (b) above is excluded by assumption). For, since in practice $x' > f'$, the first derivative of this expression with respect to i is negative.

† For inflation, by raising the value of existing physical assets relative to the value of existing financial assets, usually increases the rate at which it is necessary to acquire additional financial assets in order to maintain a given liquidity ratio; see pp. 73–5 above.

supposed, such a reduction in the payout ratio would not increase the aggregate amount of retained earnings to any significant extent (see pp. 138-9 above). For the payout ratio of the company sector, unlike the payout ratio of the individual firm, determines only the level of dividends. As a result, the beneficial effects of a reduction in the share of dividends on the fairness of the distribution of income would not be offset by an increase in the extent of capital gains on ordinary shares. Nor, for the same reason, would dividend restraint have any favourable effect (or, for that matter, any unfavourable effect) on the level of investment.

Thus in many respects dividend restriction is an attractive policy implement. There are, indeed, only two significant objections to it. One is that it would be difficult to devise a scheme of dividend restraint which did not arbitrarily penalise the shareholders of some companies more than the shareholders of other companies. The other is that the introduction of dividend restraint, which would cause a once-and-for-all drop in share prices, would discriminate unfairly against those who happened to have invested in the shares of domestic companies rather than in other forms of wealth.

(viii) *Personal taxes*

In the course of the previous chapter we defined personal taxes in a slightly unconventional way (pp. 134-5 above). For we included under this heading not only personal taxes in the ordinary sense but also the taxes paid by other sorts of owners of industrial and commercial company securities (apart from industrial and commercial companies themselves). We also established that the incidence of personal taxes is quite different from the incidence of corporation taxes on industrial and commercial companies (pp. 138-9 above). In particular, in the simplest case, in which the payout ratio and the investment coefficient are not affected by taxation, corporation taxes are completely shifted, while personal taxes on dividends, interest and capital gains are not shifted at all.

The incidence of personal taxes is not quite so simple, however, if the personal tax system discriminates between dividends and capital gains in such a way as to make the expected total personal tax bill a function of the payout ratio. For although this will have no effect on the extent of retained earnings or capital gains, it will affect the level of dividends by influencing the payout ratio. In consequence, if the personal tax system discriminates in favour of dividends, personal taxes will to some extent be shifted, since the share of dividends in national income will be larger than would otherwise have been the case. If, on the other hand, the personal tax system discriminates against dividends, the share of dividends will be lower than it would otherwise have been and thus personal taxes will be negatively shifted; that is to say, the true cost of personal taxes to shareholders will exceed the amount of tax actually paid.

Nonetheless, provided that the government appreciates the consequences of discriminating between dividends and capital gains, personal taxes provide a means by which it can exert a direct and powerful influence on the distribution of income. For as long as discrimination in favour of dividends is avoided (and in this regard it is the combined impact of the corporation tax system and the personal tax system that is relevant), the government can always reduce the net of tax shares of dividends and interest in national income by increasing the personal tax rates on these sorts of income (particularly in relation to personal tax rates on income from work), while at the same time reducing the extent of net of tax capital gains on company securities by raising the rate of capital gains tax.

Thus, simply in terms of their power to alter the distribution of income, personal taxes are markedly superior to all the other types of policy measure discussed above. In addition, personal taxes are distinctively equitable in two other respects.

(a) Personal taxes on investment income and capital gains do not discriminate unfairly between the owners of domestic company securities and those who have invested in other forms of wealth such as foreign company securities, government securities and real property.

(b) Personal taxes can be imposed in such a way as to discriminate in a desirable manner between different categories of owners of company securities. In particular, because personal taxes in the ordinary sense can (and should) be levied at a progressive rate, they enable the government to discriminate between rich and poor owners of company securities. This is important because, although the majority of company securities are owned by very wealthy people, a significant minority belong (directly and indirectly) to people who are much less well off. Similarly, the government can, if it so wishes, discriminate in favour of certain other classes of owners of company securities, such as charities and pension funds.

Finally, the government need not be inhibited from making use of personal taxes to increase the fairness of the distribution of income by fear of the consequences for the level of investment. For it is an implication of the present theory that personal taxes on dividends, interest and capital gains have virtually no effect on company sector investment. More specifically, the level of company sector investment depends only on the company sector investment coefficient, the share of the company sector in total output and the government's chosen rate of growth of aggregate demand, none of which would be significantly altered by changes in personal tax rates.*

(ix) *Other measures*

Nationalisation and the redistribution of wealth have often been suggested as ways in which the distribution of income might be made more equitable. Although the present theory bears only tangentially on these possibilities, it would be inappropriate to neglect them altogether.

(a) The nationalisation of industry has been advocated on various grounds. But if the government were to compensate share-holders fairly (and this is the principle which has been adopted in such countries as the U.K.), nationalisation would have no bene-ficial effect on the distribution of income or wealth among persons, even though it would reduce the share of profits in national income.† Moreover, no other argument for wholesale nationalisa-

---

* A change in personal taxes could affect company sector investment only if it altered the payout ratio. For this would change the company sector profit margin, which might influence the rate of growth of company sector output in one of two ways, neither of which is likely to be important in practice. (a) It might cause substitution away from or towards the products of other domestic sectors. (b) It might cause substitution away from or towards foreign products in circumstances in which the growth rate of national income was constrained by Balance of Trade considerations.

† This point is lucidly expounded in Atkinson (1972) pp. 209–18.

tion emerges from the present theory. This is not to deny, however, that there are special reasons which make it desirable that certain firms or industries should be publicly owned, and in this regard certain aspects of the present theory may be of some relevance. In particular, the case for nationalisation in specific instances may be strengthened by a more realistic view than is provided by orthodox economic theory of the financial constraints under which companies operate.

(b) The distribution of income would be improved if the distribution among persons of wealth in general and company securities in particular were made more equal. A variety of measures designed to bring this about have been proposed, of which the most advantageous, in the long run, would be an effective and progressive system for taxing all transfers of wealth between persons (see Atkinson, 1972, part II).

Such measures are sometimes opposed on the grounds that they would adversely affect investment by reducing the personal propensity to save. This may be true of investment by certain sorts of unincorporated businesses. But it is not true of company sector investment. For it follows from the present theory that an increase in the personal propensity to consume would in no way interfere with the company sector's ability to finance the investment required by any given rate of growth of demand. Nor, since governmental saving is a perfectly adequate substitute for private saving, would such an increase in the propensity to consume in a modern economy necessarily have any effect on the rate of growth of aggregate demand.

It is possible, however, that in a rather different way measures to redistribute wealth might adversely affect both company sector investment and the distribution of income. For certain measures of this kind would effectively reduce the degree of fiscal discrimination against dividends and would therefore cause an increase in the company sector payout ratio. This would raise the share of dividends in national income, which would tend to make the distribution of income less equitable. At the same time, it would raise the company sector profit margin which, by lowering the rate of growth of demand for company sector products, might lead to some slight reduction in company sector investment.

The main conclusions of this chapter can be summarised very briefly. First, there need be no conflict between making the distribution of income more equitable and maintaining or increasing the level of company sector investment. Second, such a redistribution of income could best be accomplished by judicious use of the existing tax system. In consequence, neither the wish to stimulate company sector investment nor the absence of appropriate policy implements can be used as excuses for not making the distribution of income more equitable.

REFERENCES

Annual Abstract of Statistics, Central Statistical Office, H.M.S.O. London.
Ansoff, H. I. (1965). *Corporate Strategy*, New York.
Atkinson, A. B. (1972). *Unequal Shares*, London.
Ball, R. J. (1964). *Inflation and the Theory of Money*, London.
Bank of England (1966). 'Capital issues in the United Kingdom', *Bank of England Quarterly Bulletin*, vol. VI, pp. 151–7.
Barna, T. (1962). *Investment and Growth Policies in British Industrial Firms*, Cambridge.
Baumol, W. J. (1967). *Business Behavior, Value and Growth*, New York (2nd edn).
Boulding, K. (1950). *A Reconstruction of Economics*, New York.
Brittain, J. A. (1964). 'The tax structure and corporate dividend policy', *American Economic Review, Papers and Proceedings*, vol. LIV, pp. 272–87.
Brittain, J. A. (1966). *Corporate Dividend Policy*, Washington.
Carter, C. F. and Williams, B. R. (1958). *Investment in Innovation*, London.
Coutts, K. J., Godley, W. A. H. and Nordhaus, W. D. (1975). *The Determination of Prices in U.K. Manufacturing Industry*, Cambridge, forthcoming.
Cyert, R. M. and George, K. D. (1969). 'Competition, growth and efficiency', *Economic Journal*, vol. LXXIX, pp. 23–41.
Cyert, R. M. and March, J. G. (1963). *A Behavioral Theory of the Firm*, Englewood Cliffs, N.J.
Davidson, P. (1968). 'The demand and supply of securities and economic growth', *American Economic Review, Papers and Proceedings*, vol. LVIII, pp. 252–69.
Director, The (1970). 'The why and the how of company investment', *The Director*, November, pp. 334–9.
Dougherty, C. R. S. (1972). 'On the rate of return and the rate of profit', *Economic Journal*, vol. 82, pp. 1324–50.
Downie, J. (1958). *The Competitive Process*, London.
Economic Research Group of Amsterdam – Rotterdam Bank and Other Banks (1966). *Capital Markets in Europe*, London.
Edge, S. (1965). 'Shareholders' reactions to rights issues', *Manchester School of Economic and Social Studies*, vol. XXXIII, pp. 263–84.
Eichner, A. S. (1973). 'A theory of the determination of the mark-up under oligopoly', *Economic Journal*, vol. 83, pp. 1184–200.
Ferber, R. (1967). *Determinants of Investment Behavior*, New York.
Friedman, M. (1957). *A Theory of the Consumption Function*, Princeton.
Friend, I. and Puckett, M. (1964). 'Dividends and stock prices', *American Economic Review*, vol. LIV, pp. 656–82.
Godley, W. A. H. and Nordhaus, W. D. (1972). 'Pricing in the trade cycle', *Economic Journal*, vol. 82, pp. 853–82.
Gordon, M. J. (1962). *The Investment, Financing and Valuation of the Corporation*, Homewood, Illinois.

Hahn, F. H. (1972). *The Share of Wages in the National Income*, London.
Hahn, F. H. and Matthews, R. C. O. (1965). 'The theory of economic growth', in Royal Economic Society, *Surveys of Economic Theory*, vol. II, London.
Hall, R. L. and Hitch, C. J. (1939). 'Price theory and economic behaviour', *Oxford Economic Papers*, vol. 2 (Old Series), pp. 12–46.
Harcourt, G. C. (1972). *Some Cambridge Controversies in Capital Theory*, Cambridge.
Harrod, R. F. (1939). 'An essay in dynamic theory', *Economic Journal*, vol. XLIX, pp. 14–33.
Kahn, R. F. (1959). 'Exercises in the analysis of growth', *Oxford Economic Papers*, vol. XI, pp. 143–56.
Kaldor, N. (1956). 'Alternative theories of distribution', *Review of Economic Studies*, vol. XXIII, pp. 83–100.
Kaldor, N. (1966). 'Marginal productivity and the macroeconomic theories of distribution', *Review of Economic Studies*, vol. XXXIII, pp. 309–19.
Kaldor, N. (1970a). 'On the economic effects of alternative systems of corporation tax', House of Commons Paper 622, 1970–1, App. 15.
Kaldor, N. (1970b). 'Some fallacies in the interpretation of Kaldor', *Review of Economic Studies*, vol. XXXVII (1), pp. 1–7.
Kalecki, M. (1952). *Theory of Economic Dynamics*, New York.
Keynes, J. M. (1936). *The General Theory of Employment, Interest and Money*, London.
Keynes, J. M. (1971). *A Treatise on Money*, vol. I, London (Royal Economic Society edn).
King, M. A. (1972). 'Investment incentives and taxation in a vintage investment model', *Journal of Public Economics*, vol. I, pp. 121–47.
King, M. A. (1974a). 'Dividend behaviour and the theory of the firm', *Economica*, vol. 41, pp. 25–34.
King, M. A. (1974b). 'Taxation and the cost of capital', *Review of Economic Studies*, vol. XLI(1), pp. 21–36.
Krzyzaniak, M. and Musgrave, R. (1963). *The Shifting of the Corporation Income Tax*, Baltimore.
Kuh, E. (1963). *Capital Stock Growth*, Amsterdam.
Lampman, R. (1962). *The Share of Top Wealth Holders in National Wealth*, Washington.
Leijonhufvud, A. (1969). *Keynes and the Classics*, London.
Lewellen, W. G. (1968). *Executive Compensation in Large Industrial Corporations*, New York.
Lintner, J. (1965). 'Distribution of income of corporations among dividends, retained earnings and taxes', *American Economic Review, Papers and Proceedings*, vol. XLVI, pp. 97–114.
Lintner, J. (1971). 'Optimum or maximum corporate growth under uncertainty', in R. L. Marris and A. J. B. Wood, *The Corporate Economy*, London, pp. 172–241.
Lydall, H. F. and Tipping, D. G. (1961). 'The distribution of personal wealth in Britain', *Bulletin of the Oxford University Institute of Statistics*, vol. XXIII, pp. 83–104.

Mackintosh, A. (1963). *The Development of Firms*, Cambridge.

Marris, R. L. (1964*a*). *The Economic Theory of Managerial Capitalism*, London.

Marris, R. L. (1964*b*). 'Incomes policy and the rate of profit in industry', *Transactions of the Manchester Statistical Society*, 1964–5 Session.

Marris, R. L. (1971). 'Some new results on growth and profitability', in R. L. Marris and A. J. B. Wood, *The Corporate Economy*, London, pp. 422–7.

Marris, R. L. (1972). 'Why economics needs a theory of the firm', *Economic Journal*, vol. 82, pp. 321–52.

Marris, R. L. and Wood, A. J. B. (1971). *The Corporate Economy*, London.

Marshall, A. (1949). *Principles of Economics*, London (8th edn Reset).

Marx, K. (1906). *Capital*, vol. I, New York (1st American edn).

Maurice, R. (1968). *National Accounts Statistics, Sources and Methods*, H.M.S.O., London.

Merrett, A. J., Howe, M. and Newbould, G. D. (1967). *Equity Issues and the London Capital Market*, London.

Merrett, A. J. and Sykes, A. (1964). *The Finance and Analysis of Capital Projects*, London.

Merrett, A. J. and Sykes, A. (1966). *Capital Budgeting and Company Finance*, London.

Meyer, J. and Kuh, E. (1959). *The Investment Decision*, Harvard.

Modigliani, F. and Miller, M. (1961). 'Dividend policy, growth and the valuation of shares', *Journal of Business*, vol. XXXIV, pp. 411–33.

Modigliani, F. and Miller, M. (1967). 'Estimates of the cost of capital relevant for investment decisions under uncertainty', in R. Ferber, *Determinants of Investment Behavior*, New York, pp. 179–213.

National Association of Accountants (1964). *Long Range Profit Planning*, Research Report No. 42, New York.

National Economic Development Council (1965). *Investment in Machine Tools*, H.M.S.O., London.

National Income and Expenditure (annually). Central Statistical Office, H.M.S.O., London.

Neild, R. R. (1963). *Pricing and Employment in the Trade Cycle*, Cambridge.

Neild, R. R. (1964). 'Replacement policy', *National Institute Economic Review*, vol. XXX (November), pp. 30–43.

Nerlove, M. (1968). 'Preliminary results on factors affecting differences among rates of return on investments in individual common stocks', Harvard Institute of Economic Research Paper 23.

Pasinetti, L. L. (1960). 'A mathematical formulation of the Ricardian system', *Review of Economic Studies*, vol. XXVII, pp. 78–98.

Pasinetti, L. L. (1962). 'Rate of profit and income distribution in relation to the rate of economic growth', *Review of Economic Studies*, vol. XXIX, pp. 267–79.

Reddaway, W. B. *et al.* (1967 and 1968). *Effects of U.K. Direct Investment Overseas*, Interim and Final Reports, Cambridge.

Revell, J. and Moyle, J. (1966). 'The owners of quoted ordinary shares', Published Paper 7 of 'A Programme for Growth', Department of Applied Economics, Cambridge University.

Ricardo, D. (1951). Edited by P. Sraffa. *Principles of Political Economy and Taxation*, Cambridge (Royal Economic Society edn).

Robinson, J. (1942). *An Essay in Marxian Economics*, London.

Robinson, J. (1956). *The Accumulation of Capital*, London.

Robinson, J. (1964). 'The theory of distribution', *Collected Economic Papers*, vol. II, Oxford.

Schumpeter, J. (1939). *Business Cycles*, New York.

Singh, A. (1971). *Take-overs*, Cambridge.

Singh, A. and Whittington, G. (1968). *Growth, Profitability and Valuation*, Cambridge.

Solow, R. (1968). 'The share of profits in the long and short run', in J. Marchal and B. Ducros (eds.), *The Distribution of National Income*, New York, pp. 449–66.

Steindl, J. (1952). *Maturity and Stagnation in American Capitalism*, Oxford.

Tew, B. and Henderson, R. F. (1969). *Studies in Company Finance*, Cambridge.

Turnovsky, S. J. (1967). 'The allocation of corporate profits between dividends and retained earnings', *Review of Economics and Statistics*, vol. XLIX, pp. 583–9.

Whittington, G. (1971). *The Prediction of Profitability*, Cambridge.

Williams, B. R. and Scott, W. P. (1965). *Investment Proposals and Decisions*, London.

INDEX

capital gains (*cont.*)
  and neo-Pasinetti theorem, 118n
  and new issue policy, 53–4, 56–7
  and retained earnings, 38, 156–7
  taxes, 46; incidence of, 138–9, 170–1
capital theory, Cambridge controversies, 15, 123n
Carter, C. F., 99
company sector
  definitions of variables, 105, 150–1
  distinguished from U.K. companies, 149–51
  profit margin, *see* profits, share of
  securities, new issues of, demand and supply, 118n
competition, influence of
  on company sector profit margin and share of profits in national income, 108–10
  on individual firm, 4, 65–6, 85, 86, 95, 163
  see also demand–profit margin tradeoff, monopoly *and* oligopoly
conflicts between managers and shareholders, *see* managers, interests *and* shareholders, interests of ordinary
continuity, 82, 83, 84n
cost minimisation and efficiency, 8n, 62, 66, 90, 163
Coutts, K. J., 135n
credit, *see* borrowing, lenders *and* trade credit
Cyert, R. M., 10n, 49, 61n
Davidson, P., 118n
debentures, 28
Debreu, G., 3n, 15
degree of monopoly, *see* monopoly, degree of
demand
  aggregate, 14, 64, 108, 112
  autonomous, 14, 112–13, 115, 131, 132, 141–2, 144
  for company sector products, 141–2, 145–6, 147–8
  induced, 112, 142
  for products of individual firm, 64–6, 108

demand management, 131–3, 135, 145–7, 158, 165
demand–profit margin tradeoff, 66, 67–9, 70, 84, 88
depreciation provisions, 19–20, 77, 78n, 156–7, 168
Director, The, 97
disequilibrium
  long and short run, 93, 100, 101–4, 129
  response of firm, 92–7, 100–4
  response of government, 131–2, 146
  see also equilibrium
distribution of income, *see* income distribution
dividend policy, 40–52, 77; *see also* payout ratio
dividend restraint, government-imposed, 52, 169–70
Dougherty, C. R. S., 5n
Downie, J., 10
earnings
  defined, 5
  retained, 38, 76–7, 139, 156–7, 169–70
Edge, S., 55n
efficiency, *see* cost minimisation
Eichner, A., 10n
equilibrium
  defined, 63, 82, 111, 128
  general, 15
  macroeconomic, 111, 113, 127, 128–32
  see also disequilibrium *and* growth rate, aggregate, equilibrium
emigration, 146–7
employment, *see* unemployment
expectations, subjective nature, 6, 35, 43
exports, 14n, 144–8, 169
external finance frontier, 75–6
external finance ratio
  defined, 17–19, 25, 79–80, 149, 150–1
  company sector, 105
  determinants, 75–6
  and distribution, 165–7

INDEX

subsidiaries, *see* mergers and acquisitions *and* multinational companies
taxes, 143, 160, 171, 173
  capital gains, *see* personal *in this entry*
  corporation, 20, 77, 134–8, 143–4, 147–8, 153–4, 159–60
  and dividend policy, 42–3, 46, 51, 77, 135, 137–8, 139, 159, 170–1, 173
  on dividends, *see* personal *in this entry*
  and external finance ratio, 138
  and investment coefficient, 135, 139–40, 159–60
  and leakages, 119, 131, 132
  personal, 134–5, 138–9, 170–2
  profits, incidence of, 134–40, 143–4, 147–8, 153–4, 170–1
technical progress, induced, 127–8
technique, choice of, 90, 116, 127n, 128; *see also* investment coefficient
Tew, B., 59
time, simplifying assumptions with respect to, 92n, 106
Trade, Balance of, *see* Balance of Trade
trade credit, 27n
trade, foreign, 144–8
Turnovsky, S. J., 41n, 49n

uncertainty and ignorance
  and borrowing behaviour, 5–9, 28–31
  and dividend policy, 43–6
  and Keynes, 13
  and new issue policy, 9, 55–6
  and rates of return on shares, 33–6
  and shareholding periods, 36–7
  treatment of in model of firm, 71–2
  see also disequilibrium
unemployment
  Keynesian, 124, 131, 146n
  Marxian, 124–8, 133, 142, 143, 145–7, 153, 169
unincorporated businesses, 2, 23, 140, 173
unquoted companies, 23–4, 38, 52, 53, 59–60
uses of funds account, 19, 151n
valuation ratio, 15, 38, 47, 59, 118n, 133n
value added, 107
wages
  money, 168–9
  real, 123, 124, 126, 128, 153
  relative, 142–3, 161, 162
  restraint, 168–9
Walras, L., 3n
wealth, distribution of, 3, 155, 161–2, 172–3
Whittington, G., 59n
Williams, B. R., 68n, 97, 99
yield calculations, 97–100, 119, 120–1

184